American Book Company

Meeting Standards,
Exceeding Expectations

Dear Educator,

Thank you for your interest in American Book Company's state-specific test preparation resources. We commend you for your interest in pursuing your students' success. Feel free to contact us with any questions about our books, software, or the ordering process.

Our Products Feature	Your Students Will Improve
Multiple-choice and open-ended diagnostic tests	Confidence and mastery of subjects
Step-by-step instruction	Concept development
Frequent practice exercises	Critical thinking
Chapter reviews	Test-taking skills
Multiple-choice practice tests	Problem-solving skills

American Book Company's writers and curriculum specialists have over 100 years of combined teaching experience, working with students from kindergarten through middle, high school, and adult education.

Our company specializes in effective test preparation books and software for high stakes graduation and grade promotion exams across the country.

How to Use This Book

Each book:

*contains a chart of standards which correlates all test questions and chapters to the state exam's standards and benchmarks as published by the state department of education. This chart is found in the front of all preview copies and in the front of all answer keys.

*begins with a full-length pretest (diagnostic test). This test not only adheres to your specific state standards, but also mirrors your state exam in weights and measures to help you assess each individual student's strengths and weaknesses.

*offers an evaluation chart. Depending on which questions the students miss, this chart points to which chapters individual students or the entire class need to review to be prepared for the exam.

*provides comprehensive review of all tested standards within the chapters. Each chapter includes engaging instruction, practice exercises, and chapter reviews to assess students' progress.

*finishes with two full-length practice tests for students to get comfortable with the exam and to assess their progress and mastery of the tested standards and benchmarks.

While we cannot guarantee success, our products are designed to provide students with the concept and skill development they need for the graduation test or grade promotion exam in their own state. We look forward to hearing from you soon.

Sincerely,

The American Book Company Team

PO Box 2638 ★ Woodstock, GA 30188-1383 ★ Phone: 1-888-264-5877 ★ Fax: 1-866-827-3240

Georgia 5 Writing Assessment Standards Chart

The materials in this book are based on the Georgia grade 5 scoring rubrics for writing and aligned with the GPS standards for grade 5. The following charts correlate chapters to domains and standards.

Chapter	Standards Addressed	Domains Addressed
1	ELA5C1.a, b, c	S, C
2	ELA5C1.e, f	S, C
3	ELA5W1.a	I, O, S, C
4	ELA5W1.b, c	I, O, S
5	ELA5W1.d	I, O, S
6	ELA5C1.f, g	C
7	ELA5W2.a, b, c, d, e, h, i NAR	I, O, S, C
8	ELA5W2.a, b, c, d, e, f, h, i INF	I, O, S, C
9	ELA5W2.a, b, c, d, e, f, g, h PER	I, O, S, C
10	ELA5W1, ELA5W2, ELA5C1	I, O, S, C

Chart of Standards

The following chart correlates practice essays in the Diagnostic Essay Test, Practice Essay Test 1, and Practice Essay Test 2 to the grade 5 GPS standards, published by the Georgia Department of Education, on which the writing assessment is based. These essays are also correlated with chapters in *Passing the Georgia Grade 5 Writing Assessment*.

Chapter Number	Diagnostic Essay Test Writing Prompt	Practice Essay Test 1 Writing Prompt	Practice Essay Test 2 Writing Prompt
ELA5W1 The student produces writing that establishes an appropriate organizational structure, sets a context and engages the reader, maintains a coherent focus throughout, and signals a satisfying closure. The student			
a. Selects a focus, an organizational structure, and a point of view based on purpose, genre expectations, audience, length, and format requirements.			
3	1, 2, 3	1, 2, 3	1, 2, 3
b. Writes texts of a length appropriate to address the topic or tell the story. c. Uses traditional structures for conveying information (e.g., chronological order, cause and effect, similarity and difference, and posing and answering a question).			
4	1, 2, 3	1, 2, 3	1, 2, 3
d. Uses appropriate structures to ensure coherence (e.g., transition elements).			
5	1, 2, 3	1, 2, 3	1, 2, 3

Georgia 5 Writing Assessment

Chapter Number	Diagnostic Essay Test Writing Prompt	Practice Essay Test 1 Writing Prompt	Practice Essay Test 2 Writing Prompt
ELA5W2 The student demonstrates competence in a variety of genres.			
The student produces a **narrative** that: a. Engages the reader by establishing a context, creating a point of view, and otherwise developing reader interest. b. Establishes a plot, point of view, setting, and conflict, and/or the significance of events. c. Creates an organizing structure. d. Includes sensory details and concrete language to develop plot and character. e. Excludes extraneous details and inconsistencies. h. Provides a sense of closure to the writing. i. Lifts the level of language using appropriate strategies including word choice.			
7	1	3	2
The student produces **informational** writing (e.g., report, procedures, correspondence) that: a. Engages the reader by establishing a context, creating a speaker's voice, and otherwise developing reader interest. b. Develops a controlling idea that conveys a perspective on a subject. c. Creates an organizing structure appropriate to a specific purpose, audience, and context. d. Includes appropriate facts and details. e. Excludes extraneous details and inappropriate information. f. Uses a range of appropriate strategies, such as providing facts and details, describing or analyzing the subject, and narrating a relevant anecdote. h. Provides a sense of closure to the writing. i. Lifts the level of language using appropriate strategies including word choice.			
8	2	1	3
The student produces a **persuasive** essay that: a. Engages the reader by establishing a context, creating a speaker's voice, and otherwise developing reader interest. b. States a clear position in support of a proposal. c. Supports a position with relevant evidence. d. Creates an organizing structure appropriate to a specific purpose, audience, and context. e. Addresses reader concerns. f. Excludes extraneous details and inappropriate information. g. Provides a sense of closure to the writing. h. Raises the level of language using appropriate strategies (word choice).			
9	3	2	1

Standards Chart

Chapter Number	Diagnostic Essay Test Writing Prompt	Practice Essay Test 1 Writing Prompt	Practice Essay Test 2 Writing Prompt
ELA5C1 The student demonstrates understanding and control of the rules of the English language, realizing that usage involves the appropriate application of conventions and grammar in both written and spoken formats. The student			
a. Uses and identifies the eight parts of speech (e.g., noun, pronoun, verb, adverb, adjective, conjunction, preposition, interjection). c. Uses and identifies verb phrases and verb tenses. d. Recognizes that a word performs different functions according to its position in the sentence.			
1	1, 2, 3	1, 2, 3	1, 2, 3
e. Varies the sentence structure by kind (declarative, interrogative, imperative, and exclamatory sentences and functional fragments), order, and complexity (simple, compound, complex, and compound-complex).			
2	1, 2, 3	1, 2, 3	1, 2, 3
f. Uses and identifies correct mechanics (e.g., apostrophes, quotation marks, comma use in compound sentences, paragraph indentations) and correct sentence structure (e.g., elimination of sentence fragments and run-ons).			
2, 6	1, 2, 3	1, 2, 3	1, 2, 3
g. Uses additional knowledge of correct mechanics (e.g., apostrophes, quotation marks, comma use in compound sentences, paragraph indentations), correct sentence structure (e.g., elimination of fragments and run-ons), and correct Standard English spelling (e.g., commonly used homophones) when writing, revising, and editing.			
6	1, 2, 3	1, 2, 3	1, 2, 3

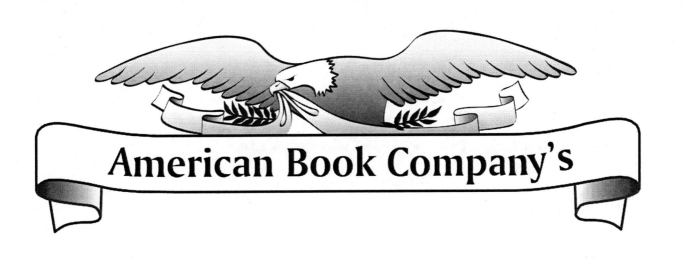

MASTERING THE

GEORGIA GRADE 5

WRITING ASSESSMENT

Sara Hinton
Kristie White Smith
Lisa M. Cocca
Zuzana Urbanek

Project Coordinator: Zuzana Urbanek
Executive Editor: Dr. Frank Pintozzi

American Book Company
PO Box 2638
Woodstock, GA 30188-1383
Toll Free: 1 (888) 264-5877 Phone: (770) 928-2834
Toll Free Fax: 1 (866) 827-3240
www.americanbookcompany.com

ACKNOWLEDGEMENTS

Special thanks goes to Dr. Karen Michael for her evaluation assistance toward the development of this book.

The authors would like to gratefully acknowledge the editing assistance of Mallory Grantham and the formatting and technical contributions of Marsha Torrens.

We also want to thank Rachae Brooks for developing the graphics for this book.

Table of Contents

PREFACE

About the Book

Mastering the Georgia Grade 5 Writing Assessment will help students who are reviewing for the Georgia Grade 5 Writing Assessment. The materials in this book are based on the Georgia grade 5 scoring rubrics for writing and aligned with the GPS standards for grade 5. The book is written at the fifth-grade level, corresponding to approximately 750L to 950L on the Lexile text measure scale.

This book contains several sections, including 1) general information about the book, 2) a diagnostic test section of sample writing prompts, 3) a diagnostic evaluation chart, 4) ten chapters that teach the concepts and skills needed for test readiness, 5) two practice tests of writing prompts, and 6) appendices of additional writing prompts and other resources.

Standards and domains covered in each chapter are posted at the beginning of the chapter and in a chart included in the answer manual.

We welcome comments and suggestions about the book. Please contact us at:

American Book Company
PO Box 2638
Woodstock, GA 30188-1383

Toll Free: 1 (888) 264-5877
Phone: (770) 928-2834
Fax: (770) 928-7483
Web site: www.americanbookcompany.com

About the Authors

Sara Hinton has a B.A. from Columbia University and an M.A. in The Teaching of English from Teachers College, Columbia University. She taught middle school language arts and college courses in writing, grammar, and literature for several years.

Kristie White Smith is a language arts teacher in the Georgia Public School System. Since 2000, she has taught a variety of language arts and English courses ranging from the middle grades through the college level. Her Ed.S. degree is from Mercer University.

Lisa M. Cocca is a former elementary and middle school teacher and librarian. She writes language arts, social studies, and science materials for a wide range of ages.

Zuzana Urbanek serves as ELA Curriculum Coordinator for American Book Company. She is a professional writer with twenty-five years of experience in education, business, and publishing. She has taught a variety of English courses since 1990 at the college level and also taught English as a foreign language abroad. Her master's degree is from Arizona State University.

About the Executive Editor

Dr. Frank J. Pintozzi is a former Professor of Education at Kennesaw State University. For over twenty-eight years, he has taught English and reading at the high school and college levels as well as in teacher preparation courses in language arts and social studies. In addition to writing and editing state standard-specific texts for school exit and end of course exams, he has edited and written numerous college textbooks.

Preparing for the Georgia Grade 5 Writing Assessment

Finally, you're a fifth grader. Your year will be an adventure!

Along with the fun of school-wide activities and class celebrations, you will have new academic responsibility. One challenge that you will have this year is the Grade 5 Writing Assessment. This test will measure what you have learned about the writing process. When you take the test, you will be given a topic, tools for writing, and a time limit. Then, as you have done in your classrooms before, you will use what you know about the writing process to write a response.

Let's take a look at some ways you can prepare for the Grade 5 Writing Assessment.

What will I write?

On test day, you will be given a *prompt*. A prompt is simply a question or topic statement. The writing prompt will be your topic for writing. Based on the prompt, you will then write a response using one of three types of writing—informational, narrative, or persuasive. If the writing is informational, it will give facts about a subject. If the prompt calls for narrative writing, then you will tell a story about something. Finally, if the writing is persuasive, you will write to convince your reader about something. In your class and in this book, you will learn how to understand the cues that will let you know what type of writing to do.

How much time will I have?

The Grade 5 Writing Assessment is a *timed test*. This means that you will have a set amount of time to complete your response. The important thing is to use your time wisely and to pace yourself for each portion of the writing process. The following is a timeline to help you stay on track and ensure that you have enough time to finish an effective response. You can use this timeline to help yourself practice writing at home and in the classroom.

Planning/Prewriting: **15 minutes**

During this time, you will decide what to write. You will use brainstorming or freewriting to generate ideas. You will think quickly to come up with as many ideas as possible. Then, you will organize your ideas and decide what each paragraph will focus on.

Drafting: **45 minutes**

You will write your paper in its entirety. In doing so, you will use the best ideas you generated during the planning/pre-writing phase.

Revising/Editing: **20 minutes**

Now, you will read over what you've drafted. You will revise for organization, making sure that all of your details relate to the main idea. You will add any ideas that are missing, delete anything repetitive or unneeded, improve word choice, and so on. You can also edit any errors in grammar, punctuation, and spelling that you find.

Final Draft: **30 minutes**

You will write your final draft neatly. In doing so, you will consider all of the adjustments you have made.

Proofreading: **10 minutes**

After writing your final draft, you will proofread for errors in grammar, punctuation, sentence formation, and spelling. This is your final review to ensure that your finished work is your best.

What can I do to ensure that I score my best?

When it comes time to take the writing assessment, you will want to do your very best. Here are a few tips to help you:

1. **Listen and prepare well in class**. Your classroom teacher is your resident expert. If you listen, pay attention, and do your best work all year long, the writing assessment will be just like another day in the classroom. You will feel confident and will score well.

2. **Practice, practice, practice**. Have you ever heard someone say that practice makes perfect? Well, this idea certainly can be applied to your writing. The more you work at it, the more natural it will become. Practice in class. Practice at home. Practice until you are comfortable.

3. **Be smart about your health.** Start test day (and every day) right. Sleep well—get a good night's rest. Eat well—get a good breakfast. This will help you to focus with a clear mind on test day and every day.

4. **Relax.** When test day comes, relax and feel confident that you have worked hard to prepare yourself. Your preparation will pay off!

Georgia 5 Writing Assessment Diagnostic Essay Test

Imagine that you are taking the Georgia Grade 5 Writing Assessment today. How would you do? What score might your essay get? This diagnostic test can help you answer these questions. It can show you where you would do well and what you need to work on. The practice essay is based on the Georgia grade 5 scoring rubrics and writing standards.

When you take the Grade 5 Writing Assessment, you will write one essay based on one writing prompt. You won't know what kind of prompt you will get. So, to get the best practice, you should write each kind of essay that you might need to write for the test: narrative, informational, and persuasive. There is one prompt for each type of essay in this diagnostic test. You don't need to write them all on the same day. Practice one now and the others at another time.

How to Use Your Time

To use your time wisely, follow these suggestions:

Planning/Prewriting (15 minutes)

During this time, you will decide what to write. You will use brainstorming or freewriting to generate ideas. You will think quickly to come up with as many ideas as possible. Then, you will organize your ideas and decide what each paragraph will focus on.

Drafting (45 minutes)

You will write your paper in its entirety. In doing so, you will use the best ideas you generated during the planning/prewriting phase.

Revising/Editing (20 minutes)

Now, you will read over what you've drafted. You will revise for organization, making sure that all of your details relate to the main idea. You will add any ideas that are missing, delete anything repetitive or unneeded, improve word choice, and so on. You can also edit any errors in grammar, punctuation, and spelling that you find.

Final Draft (30 minutes)

You will write your final draft neatly. In doing so, you will consider all of the adjustments you have made.

Proofreading (10 minutes)

After writing your final draft, you will proofread for errors in grammar, punctuation, sentence formation, and spelling. This is your final review to ensure that your finished work is your best.

When you are finished with your essay, work with your teacher or tutor to score it. Use the scoring rubrics in chapter 10. Also, fill in the **Writing Progress Chart** in Appendix C. It will help you learn your strengths and weaknesses and to track your progress.

Here are the writing prompts. Use the writing checklist for each prompt to make sure you have not forgotten anything. When you take the writing assessment, you will receive such a checklist. Use your own paper to plan, draft, revise, and edit. Write a final copy on one clean sheet of paper. Ask your teacher or tutor to tell you when to start and stop writing. Do your best, and remember: this is your first try. As you study the chapters in this book and practice writing, you will have time to improve.

Writing Prompt 1

Congratulations! You will take part in a new television show. As part of the show, you will live alone on a deserted island for two weeks. There is no electricity, no Internet, and no television. Your will receive plenty to eat and a place to live. The bad news is you may only bring three personal items with you. Write a story telling what three items you would take. Tell why you chose those items and how you would use those items.

Student Writing Checklist for Narrative Writing

☐ **Prepare Yourself to Write**
Read the writing topic carefully.
Brainstorm for ideas using your imagination and/or personal experiences.
Decide what ideas to include and how to organize them.
Write only in English.

☐ **Make Your Paper Meaningful**
Use your imagination and/or personal experiences to provide specific details.
Tell a complete story.
Create a plot or order of events.
Describe the setting and characters in your story.
Write a story that has a beginning, middle, and end.

☐ **Make Your Paper Interesting to Read**
Think about what would be interesting to the reader.
Use a lively writing voice that holds the interest of your reader.
Use descriptive words.
Use different types of sentences.

☐ **Make Your Paper Easy to Read**
Write in paragraph form.
Use transition words.
Write in complete and correct sentences.
Capitalize, spell, and punctuate correctly.
Make sure your subjects and verbs agree.

Writing Prompt 2

> Your friend wants to learn how to make a sandwich. Think about a sandwich you know how to make. Write a report explaining to your friend how to make the sandwich. Remember to tell your friend what ingredients and tools you need to make the sandwich and what steps you need to follow to make it.

Student Writing Checklist for Informational Writing

☐ **Prepare Yourself to Write**
Read the writing topic carefully.
Brainstorm for ideas.
Decide what ideas to include and how to organize them.
Write only in English.

☐ **Make Your Paper Meaningful**
Use your knowledge and/or personal experiences that are related to the topic.
Explain your ideas.
Develop your main idea with supporting details.
Organize your ideas in a clear order.
Write an informational paper and stay on topic.

☐ **Make Your Paper Interesting to Read**
Think about what would be interesting to the reader.
Use a lively writing voice to hold the interest of your reader.
Use descriptive words.
Use different types of sentences.

☐ **Make Your Paper Easy to Read**
Write in paragraph form.
Use transition words.
Write in complete and correct sentences.
Capitalize, spell, and punctuate correctly.
Make sure your subjects and verbs agree.

Writing Prompt 3

Your class will go on one field trip this month. Your teacher wants suggestions from you and your classmates about where to go. Write an essay to persuade your teacher to pick your choice for the fieldtrip. Tell where you would like to go and give three reasons for your choice.

Student Writing Checklist for Persuasive Writing

☐ **Prepare Yourself to Write**
Read the writing topic carefully.
Brainstorm for ideas.
Decide what ideas to include and how to organize them.
Write only in English.

☐ **Make Your Paper Meaningful**
Use your knowledge and/or personal experiences that are related to the topic.
Express a clear point of view.
Use details, examples, and reasons to support your point of view.
Organize your ideas in a clear order.
Write a persuasive paper and stay on topic.

☐ **Make Your Paper Interesting to Read**
Think about what would be interesting to your reader.
Use a lively writing voice to hold the interest of your reader.
Use descriptive words.
Use different types of sentences.

☐ **Make Your Paper Easy to Read**
Write in paragraph form.
Use transition words.
Write in complete and correct sentences.
Capitalize, spell, and punctuate correctly.
Make sure your subjects and verbs agree.

Chapter 1
Working with Words

This chapter addresses the Grade 5 Writing Assessment Style and Conventions rubrics and covers the following GPS standard:

> **ELA5C1 The student demonstrates understanding and control of the rules of the English language, realizing that usage involves the appropriate application of conventions and grammar in both written and spoken formats. The student**
>
> a. Uses and identifies the eight parts of speech (e.g., noun, pronoun, verb, adverb, adjective, conjunction, preposition, interjection).
>
> c. Uses and identifies verb phrases and verb tenses.
>
> d. Recognizes that a word performs different functions according to its position in the sentence.

Do you remember when you learned to speak? Do you remember being taught to put words together in a way that makes sense? Probably not. You began learning to speak and put words together very early in your life. By now, you don't even realize that you are somewhat of an expert at this. You use words in a more complex way than you ever realize. This chapter is about working with words. Here, we will take a look at the way words function in the sentences that we use. Let's begin with the parts of speech.

PARTS OF SPEECH

We use words to communicate. When we speak, read, or write, words are the building blocks that are used to create our messages. If we think of these words as being a part of a team, then it is important to note that every team member—every word—has a role to play in the job of communication.

The way that words work in a sentence explains their **parts of speech**. There are eight parts of speech. Each one is important to convey messages through speaking, reading, or writing. Now, we will take a look at each of the eight parts of speech.

NOUNS

A **noun** is a word that names a person, place, thing, or idea.

> **Example:** The <u>boy</u> went to <u>school</u> on the <u>bus</u>.

In this sentence, *boy*, *school*, and *bus* are all nouns. A boy is a person. School is a place and thing. A bus is also a thing.

> **Example:** The <u>police officer</u> showed <u>courage</u> when he rescued the <u>child</u>.

In this sentence, *police officer*, *courage*, and *child* are all nouns.

A police officer is a person. Courage is an idea. A child is also a person.

> **Example:** The <u>desert's</u> dry <u>heat</u> was hard to survive.

In this sentence, *desert* and *heat* are nouns.

A desert is a place. Heat is a thing.

Take a look at the chart for a few more examples.

Nouns			
Persons	**Places**	**Things**	**Ideas**
George Washington	Mount Vernon	house	patriotism
Maya Angelou	St. Louis	book	hope
Amy Tan	California	war	freedom
student	beach	sun block	fun
clerk	park	CD	love

PRONOUNS

A **pronoun** is a word used in the place of one or more nouns.

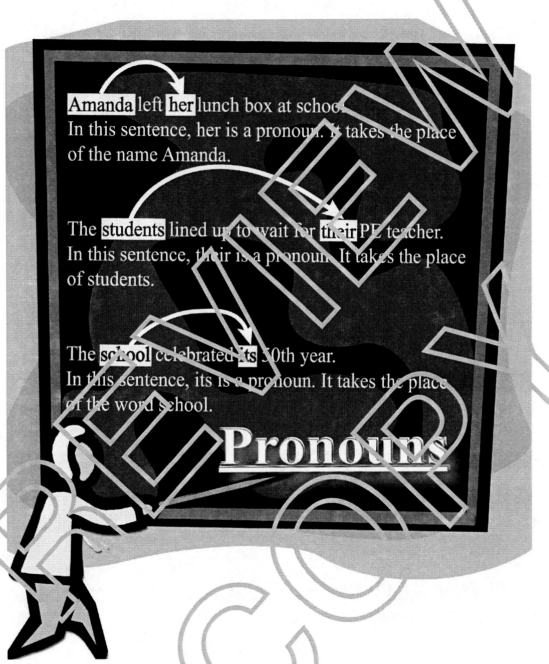

Amanda left her lunch box at school.
In this sentence, her is a pronoun. It takes the place of the name Amanda.

The students lined up to wait for their PE teacher.
In this sentence, their is a pronoun. It takes the place of students.

The school celebrated its 50th year.
In this sentence, its is a pronoun. It takes the place of the word school.

Pronouns

See the following charts for more examples of pronouns.

PERSONAL PRONOUNS

A **personal pronoun** refers to a specific person, place, or thing.

	Singular	**Plural**
First Person	I, me, my, mine	we, us, our, ours
Second Person	you, your, yours	you, your, yours
Third Person	he, him, his, she, her, hers, it, its	they, them, their, theirs

REFLEXIVE AND INTENSIVE PRONOUNS

Reflexive pronouns are the same as **intensive pronouns**. They are called reflexive when they refer back to the subject of sentence (Rob kept the biggest apple for *himself*). They are called intensive when they emphasize their antecedent (Queen Elizabeth *herself* attended the ceremony).

First Person	myself, ourselves	we, us, our, ours
Second Person	yourself, yourselves	you, your, yours
Third Person	himself, herself, itself, themselves	they, them, their, theirs

DEMONSTRATIVE PRONOUNS

A **demonstrative pronoun** points to and identifies something. "This" and "these" refer to things that are nearby in time or space (This is a bad movie). "That" and "those" refer to things that are farther away (That was a great meal).

Nearby	**Farther Away**
this	that
these	those

INTERROGATIVE PRONOUNS

An **interrogative pronoun** is used to ask a question.

what	whom
which	whose
who	

RELATIVE PRONOUNS

A **relative pronoun** can be used to link phrases or clauses.

that	which	whom
what	who	whose

COMMON INDEFINITE PRONOUNS

An **indefinite pronoun** refers to something or someone not specified. It conveys the idea of "someone" or "something."

all	anyone	either	few	nobody	some
another	anything	everybody	many	none	somebody
any	both	everyone	most	no one	someone
anybody	each	everything	neither	nothing	something

VERBS

A **verb** is a word used to express action or state of being.

> **Example:** The frogs <u>hopped</u> across the marshy bank.

In this sentence, *hopped* is a word that expresses the action of frogs.

> **Example:** Daniel and Malik <u>skateboard</u> down the block.

In this sentence, *skateboard* is a word that expresses action.

> **Example:** I <u>am</u> really tired.

In this sentence, the verb is *am*. It is what is called a "state of being" verb. State of being verbs are forms of the verb *to be*. The following are other state of being verbs: is, are, was, were, be, being, been.

ADVERBS

An **adverb** is a word used to describe or add details to a verb, an adjective, or another adverb. Adverbs tell where, when, how, how much, and to what extent.

> **Example:** We will camp <u>here</u> for the night.

Here is an adverb. It tells where we will camp for the night.

> **Example:** I will get my homework done <u>today</u>.

Today is an adverb. It tells when I will get homework done.

> **Example:** The boy ran <u>quickly</u> to escape the rain.

Quickly is an adverb. It tells how the boy ran.

> **Example:** The children were <u>very</u> tired after a day at the zoo.

Very is an adverb. It tells the extent of the children's tiredness.

ADJECTIVES

An **adjective** is a word used to describe or add details to a noun or pronoun. An adjective tells what kind, which one, how much, or how many. The most commonly used adjectives are *a, and*, and *the*. These are called **articles**. Let's take a look at some examples.

> **Example:** The <u>hairy</u> beast roared, scaring the villagers away.

Hairy is an adjective in this sentence. It tells what kind of beast.

> **Example:** <u>That</u> house on the corner belongs to me.

In this sentence, *that* is an adjective. It adds details to the noun *house* and tells which one.

> **Example:** It takes <u>less</u> time to walk to the park than it does to walk to the zoo.

In this sentence, *less* is an adjective. It adds details to the noun time and tells how much.

CONJUNCTIONS

A **conjunction** is a word used to join words or groups of words.

> **Example:** Bobbie <u>and</u> Allie walk to school together.

In this sentence, *and* joins Bobbie with Allie.

> **Example:** Shelly likes peanut butter, <u>but</u> she doesn't like jelly.

In this sentence, *but* joins the short sentence "Shelly likes peanut butter" with the short sentence "she doesn't like jelly."

> **Example:** Scott woke up late, <u>so</u> he was late to school.

In this sentence, *so* joins the short sentence "Scott woke up late" with the short sentence "he was late to school."

PREPOSITIONS

A **preposition** is a word used to show the relationship of a noun or a pronoun to another word in the sentence. Notice how prepositions in each of the following sentences are used.

> **Examples:** My homework is <u>in</u> my backpack.
> The cat ran <u>under</u> the table.
> The girl stood <u>next to</u> her mother.
> The crying boy ran <u>behind</u> his older brother.
> Across the field is a path <u>to</u> the old fire station.

INTERJECTIONS

An **interjection** is a word used to express emotion. It is often followed by an exclamation mark.

> **Examples:** <u>Wow!</u> Donovan got a cell phone for his birthday.
>
> <u>Ouch!</u> That soup is still very hot.
>
> <u>Aha!</u> I've solved the puzzle.

In the sentences above, the words *wow*, *ouch*, and *aha* are interjections. They express strong emotion. *Wow* expresses surprise and the feeling of being impressed. *Ouch* is used to express pain. *Aha* is used to express pride at the accomplishment of a job well done.

Practice 1: Parts of Speech

ELA5C1.a

Read each sentence. Then, choose the letter that matches the part of speech for the underlined word.

1. Don't tell <u>my</u> sister that I was late for math.
   A. noun   B. pronoun   C. verb   D. adverb

2. I <u>often</u> dream about being in a room full of ice cream and balloons.
   A. adjective   B. adverb   C. preposition   D. interjection

3. There are <u>many</u> career choices in the computer industry.
   A. adjective   B. verb   C. interjection   D. conjunction

4. I love strawberry ice cream, <u>and</u> chocolate is my second favorite.
   A. adjective   B. adverb   C. preposition   D. conjunction

5. <u>Whew!</u> I almost forgot my homework.
   A. adjective   B. verb   C. interjection   D. conjunction

6. <u>Myra</u> made a list of the things she had to do.
   A. noun   B. pronoun   C. interjection   D. preposition

7. The birds flew <u>over</u> the field of wild flowers.
   A. noun   B. pronoun   C. interjection   D. preposition

8. Will you <u>return</u> my library books?
   A. verb   B. noun   C. adverb   D. interjection

WORD POSITIONS

When you look to identify parts of speech, consider how and where the word is used in the sentence. This is important because **word position** affects part of speech. Let's look at some examples of how word position can affect part of speech.

Examples: After working for thirty years, the elementary teacher <u>retired</u>.

The <u>retired</u> elementary teacher found herself wanting to go back to the classroom.

In the first sentence, *retired* is a verb. It is an action. However, in the second sentence, the same word, *retired*, is an adjective that describes the elementary teacher.

Example: The children <u>skate</u> across the rink.

Samantha's left <u>skate</u> began to hurt her ankle.

In the first sentence, *skate* is a verb. It is an action. In the second sentence, *skate* is a noun. It is a thing.

Example: I <u>love</u> to visit my family in Budapest.

Reading is my greatest <u>love</u>.

In the first sentence, *love* is a verb. However, in the second sentence, *love* is a noun.

Practice 2: Word Position

ELA5C1.c

Read each sentence. Then, decide how the underlined word is being used.

1. The <u>soccer</u> field is wet from yesterday's rain.
    A. noun   B. verb   C. adverb   D. adjective

2. We play <u>soccer</u> in a local league.
    A. noun   B. verb   C. adverb   D. adjective

3. The curious puppy wandered out into the <u>cold</u>.
    A. preposition   B. adjective   C. noun   D. conjunction

4. The <u>cold</u> ice cream was a great treat in the summer heat.
    A. noun   B. adjective   C. interjection   D. verb

5. The fifth graders' <u>chant</u> could be heard from across the field.
    A. verb   B. interjection   C. noun   D. preposition

6. The preschool children loudly <u>chant</u> the days of the week.
    A. verb   B. interjection   C. noun   D. preposition

MORE ABOUT VERBS

Earlier in the chapter, we looked at verbs as a part of speech. Again, verbs are words that express action or a state of being. Sometimes, verbs are used as part of a phrase. A **verb phrase** consists of a main verb and its **helping verbs** (verbs that help the main verb to do its job of expressing action or state of being). Let's look at some examples.

> Monica *has been awarded* for her bravery with the Girl Scout troop

> The tutoring lesson *may take* longer than one hour.

> I *did* not *earn* my allowance last week.

In these examples, *has been*, *may*, and *did* are all helping verbs.

Another thing to note about verbs is the idea of tense. **Verb tense** identifies when an action takes place. The three basic verb tenses are **past**, **present**, and **future**.

Let's look at some verbs and how they change tenses.

BASIC VERB TENSES		
Past	**Present**	**Future**
I ate	I eat	I will eat
I slept	I sleep	I will sleep
I dreamt	I dream	I will dream
I wrote	I write	I will write

Practice 3. Verb Tenses and Phrases

ELA5C1.b

Read each sentence. Then, decide whether the underlined verb uses the past, present, or future tense.

1. Yesterday, we <u>drove</u> to the city.
   A. past   B. present   C. future

2. I <u>dream</u> of one day becoming a singer.
   A. past   B. present   C. future

3. We <u>will work</u> on math for two periods today.
   A. past   B. present   C. future

For questions 4 through 6, choose the correct verb form to complete each sentence.

4. I _____ this morning and missed my bus. Now, I am late for school. (past tense)
    A. oversleep   B. overslept   C. will oversleep

5. I _____ pepperoni pizza. (present tense)
    A. love   B. will love   C. loved

6. I _____ my rain coat at school today. (past tense)
    A. leave   B. left   C. will leave

CHAPTER 1 SUMMARY

A **noun** is a word that names a person, place, thing, or idea.

A **pronoun** is a word used in the place of one or more nouns.

A **verb** is a word used to express action or state of being.

An **adverb** is a word used to describe or add details to a verb, an adjective, or another adverb. Adverbs tell where, when, how, how much, and to what extent.

An **adjective** is a word used to describe or add details to a noun or pronoun. An adjective tells what kind, which one, how much, or how many. The most commonly used adjectives are the **articles** *a, and*, and *the*.

A **conjunction** is a word used to join words or groups of words.

A **preposition** is a word used to show the relationship of a noun or a pronoun to another word.

An **interjection** is a word used to express emotion. It is often followed by an exclamation mark. When you look to identify parts of speech, consider **word position** and how it affects part of speech.

A **verb phrase** consists of a main verb and its **helping verbs**—verbs that help the main verb to do its job of expressing action or state of being.

Verb tense identifies when an action takes place. Three basic verb tenses are **past**, **present**, and **future** tense.

CHAPTER 1 REVIEW

ELA5C1.a, c, d

Read questions 1 through 12. Choose the correct part of speech for the underlined word.

1. The cheerleading squad spent hours at <u>Saturday</u> practice.
   A. noun   B. verb   C. adjective   D. interjection

2. <u>Hey!</u> That boy lives in my old neighborhood.
   A. noun   B. verb   C. adjective   D. interjection

3. The brown mouse scurried <u>across</u> the kitchen floor.
   A. preposition   B. conjunction   C. verb   D. pronoun

4. The young ballerina <u>was</u> a diamond in the rough.
   A. noun   B. verb   C. adjective   D. pronoun

5. I love to dance <u>and</u> sing.
   A. conjunction   B. noun   C. interjection   D. verb

6. Martin rubbed the sore spot on <u>his</u> elbow.
   A. noun   B. pronoun   C. verb   D. interjection

7. The toddler scowled <u>angrily</u> as his mother put him down for a nap.
   A. noun   B. pronoun   C. adverb   D. conjunction

8. The <u>sunshine</u> warmed her face, arms, and legs.
   A. noun   B. pronoun   C. adverb   D. conjunction

9. We <u>play</u> hopscotch in the cul-de-sac after school.
   A. noun   B. pronoun   C. adverb   D. verb

10. Mack's <u>iPod</u> is his prized possession.
    A. noun   B. pronoun   C. adverb   D. verb

11. The display of <u>Asian</u> art was stunning and beautiful.
    A. adjective   B. interjection   C. adverb   D. preposition

12. I will not walk <u>across</u> the boulevard without my older sister.
    A. adjective   B. interjection   C. adverb   D. preposition

For questions 13 through 15, decide the verb tense of the underlined verb in the sentence.

13. Last year, our class <u>took</u> a trip to the coast.
    A. present   B. past   C. future

14. We <u>buy</u> hot dogs and soda from the corner stand.
    A. present   B. past   C. future

15. Next year, we <u>will be</u> middle school students.
    A. present   B. past   C. future

For questions 16 through 20, identify the verb phrase in each sentence.

16. The fifth graders should be in PE by now.
    A. graders should   C. should be
    B. be in PE   D. none of these

17. Do not look back at the sun.
    A. do not look   C. look back
    B. do look   D. do look back

18. How will we know the number of jelly beans that are in the jar?
    A. will know   C. beans that are
    B. how will we   D. in the jar

19. The driver could have decided to wait for the tardy student.
    A. the driver could   C. could have decided
    B. for the student   D. driver could have

20. My sprained ankle has been giving me problems for a while.
    A. has been   C. ankle has been
    B. has been giving   D. my sprained

Chapter 2
Using Sentences

This chapter addresses the Grade 5 Writing Assessment Style and Conventions rubrics and covers the following GPS standard:

ELA5C1 The student demonstrates understanding and control of the rules of the English language, realizing that usage involves the appropriate application of conventions and grammar in both written and spoken formats. The student

    e. Varies the sentence structure by kind (declarative, interrogative, imperative, and exclamatory sentences and functional fragments), order, and complexity (simple, compound, complex, and compound-complex).

    f. Uses and identifies correct mechanics (e.g., apostrophes, quotation marks, comma use in compound sentences, paragraph indentations) and correct sentence structure (e.g., elimination of sentence fragments and run-ons).

In the last chapter, we looked at words and how they play roles as parts of speech in a sentence. When groups of words form complete ideas, they become sentences. In this chapter, we will explore different kinds of sentence types and how they communicate ideas. We will also practice sentence punctuation. Let's begin with sentence types.

TYPES OF SENTENCES

A **sentence** is a word group that makes a complete thought. It contains a **subject** (what the sentence is about) and a **predicate** (what the subject is or does). There are four basic categories that group sentences according to their purpose. These categories are: declarative, interrogative, imperative, and exclamatory. Let's look at each one.

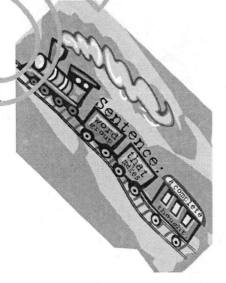

A **declarative** sentence makes a statement. It gives information. Here are some examples.

> Today is a very humid day.
> The line in the cafeteria is very long.
> I will go to bed early tonight.

The next basic sentence type is interrogative. An **interrogative** sentence asks a question. It ends with a question mark. Here are some examples.

> Did you complete the homework assignment?
>
> Will you please get your chores done early?
>
> Why are you eating so slowly?

Imperative sentences give commands. They make requests to have something done.

> Go to the store.
>
> Take your books upstairs to your bedroom.
>
> Sit down in the third row.

Exclamatory sentences show excitement. They are punctuated with an exclamation mark.

> It is snowing in July!
>
> That cat look like it weighs fifty pounds!
>
> You ate the last chocolate ice cream bar!

Practice 1: Types of Sentences

ELA5C1.e

Read each sentence. Then, choose the letter that matches the sentence type.

1. Go to your room, and work on your book report.

   A. declarative   B. interrogative   C. imperative   D. exclamatory

2. There are 365 days in a year.

   A. declarative   B. interrogative   C. imperative   D. exclamatory

3. The house is on fire!

   A. declarative

   B. interrogative

   C. imperative

   D. exclamatory

4. Will you hand me the butter?

   A. declarative

   B. interrogative

   C. imperative

   D. exclamatory

CLAUSES

Another important part of working with sentences is being able to identify a sentence's different parts, such as clauses and phrases. Let's look at clauses first.

A **clause** is a group of words that contains a verb and its subject. It is used as a part of a sentence. For example:

> The girls gathered to remember their friend Patricia.
>
> I wanted to go to the movies today.
>
> I will not repeat what I said.
>
> Since you ate my dessert yesterday, I will eat your slice of pizza today.

There are two kinds of clauses—independent and dependent. An **independent clause** expresses a complete thought. It can stand alone as a sentence. For example:

> After breakfast, I left for school.
>
> Since it was Friday, there would be a test.
>
> Hannah brought the Goldfish crackers, and I brought the grapes.

Unlike independent clauses, **dependent clauses** do not express a complete thought and cannot stand alone as sentences. Words such as *that*, *what*, or *since* often signal the beginning of a dependent clause. A dependent clause is also called a **subordinate clause**. Let's look at some examples.

> At the library, I found the book that I wanted.
>
> Since I forgot to study, I failed my math test.
>
> The scared girl could not explain what she had seen in the cave.

Practice 2: Clauses

ELA5C1.e

Decide whether each of the following underlined clauses is dependent or independent.

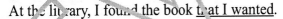

1. Monica remembered <u>what her grandmother taught her</u> about strangers.
   A. dependent   B. independent

2. <u>Terrence walked home</u> with the sound of city traffic whizzing in his ears.
   A. dependent   B. independent

3. <u>Kunal sat still</u>, trying to listen to his parents speaking in the kitchen.
   A. dependent   B. independent

4. <u>Since Brooke had moved away</u>, Sheila no longer had a best friend in town.
   A. dependent   B. independent

Understanding clauses will help you to understand about **sentence structure**. When we think of structure, we think of how words in a sentence fit together. We will now look at four sentence structures: simple, compound, complex, and compound-complex. Let's begin with simple sentences.

SIMPLE SENTENCES

A **simple sentence** has one independent clause and no dependent clauses. Here are some examples.

> The boy looked around the room.
>
> The grass was greener on the other side.
>
> Hector and Marcello played computer games after school.

COMPOUND SENTENCES

Sometimes, two or more simple sentences are joined together. When this happens, a **compound sentence** is formed. Compound sentences do not have subordinate clauses. Look at these examples.

> The weather is turning, and leaves are falling from the trees.
>
> The girl was hungry, so she ate some yogurt.
>
> Kenya laughed, but Olivia cried.

Use commas before the conjunctions in compound sentences. Common conjunctions are *for, and, nor, but, or, yet,* and *so.* These are easy to remember if you remember "fanboys," spelled out by the first letter of each conjunction.

COMPLEX SENTENCES

A **complex sentence** has one independent clause plus one or more dependent clauses. Here are some examples.

> Even though he thought it would never happen in Florida, Kevin wished for a snow day.

independent clause: Kevin wished for a snow day

dependent clause: even though he thought it would never happen

> When Jacques practiced his cello every day, he became a better player.

independent clause: he became a better player

dependent clause: when Jacques practiced his cello every day

COMPOUND-COMPLEX SENTENCES

Now, you have reviewed compound sentences and complex sentence. So, you can probably guess what a compound-complex sentence is. A **compound-complex sentence** has two or more independent clauses plus at least one dependent clause. As you look at the following examples, try to identify the clauses in the sentences.

> Federico would not look away from the television, but he continued to reach for a cookie from the glass jar that was on the edge of the counter.

independent clause: Federico would not look away from the television

independent clause: he continued to reach for a cookie

dependent clause: that was on the edge of the counter

> She had not done her homework, so Lily sat at her desk and looked out the window at her friends who were playing nearby.

independent clause: she had not done her homework

independent clause: Lily sat at her desk and looked out the window at her friends

dependent clause: who were playing nearby

Practice 3: Sentences

ELA5C1.e

Read each sentence. Decide what type of sentence you see.

1. Michelle counted the money she made.

   A. simple

   B. compound

   C. complex

   D. compound-complex

2. We did our homework, and we waited for our parents to return home.

   A. simple

   B. compound

   C. complex

   D. compound-complex

3. Since Ms. Stiller was out sick, her fifth grade class decided they needed a break from the norm, and they did not follow the usual classroom rules.

   A. simple
   B. compound
   C. complex
   D. compound-complex

4. If you want to be successful, you must work very hard, and you must be responsible.

   A. simple
   B. compound
   C. complex
   D. compound-complex

FRAGMENTS AND RUN-ONS

As you continue to learn about sentence structure, you will see that there are many common sentence errors. Two common errors are fragments and run-ons. Let's look at fragments first.

A **fragment** is a group of words that is punctuated like a sentence but that lacks a subject, predicate, or both. Let's look at some examples of fragments.

> Went to the park. (Who went to the park? The subject is missing.)
>
> Andrew's shoes. (This could be a subject, but what is the predicate?)
>
> From the other side of the street. (What is the subject? What is the predicate?)

Run-ons occur when a writer joins two or more complete sentences without using proper punctuation or without a conjunction.

> Joey went around the corner to the deli he wanted to get a roast beef hoagie.

There are two complete sentences here. There are three ways to correct this error.

1. **Turn the run-on into two separate sentences.** A period must follow each sentence.

   Joey went around the corner to the deli. He wanted to get a roast beef hoagie.

2. **Another solution is to use a semicolon between the dependent clauses.**

   Joey went around the corner to the deli; he wanted to get a roast beef hoagie.

3. **Yet another way to join the sentences is to use a comma and a conjunction.**

   Joey went around the corner to the deli, as he wanted to get a roast beef hoagie.

Here are three more examples of this sentence error. On your own paper, write two or three correct ways to revise each run-on.

> Can you bring me my raincoat it is raining today.
>
> I am really tired, I ran all the way home.
>
> She brought us cookies and cupcakes they were delicious!

Practice 4: Fragments and Run-ons

ELA5C1.f

Read each word group. Decide if the group of words is a fragment, run-on, or correct as a complete sentence.

1. The dogs slept lazily in the autumn sun.

   A. fragment   B. run-on   C. correct

2. My ears popped in the elevator we went to the fifteenth floor.

   A. fragment   B. run-on   C. correct

3. When it is raining outside and clouds are filling up the sky.

   A. fragment   B. run-on   C. correct

4. Since yesterday when we went shopping at the mall.

   A. fragment   B. run-on   C. correct

MECHANICS

There is a technical side to writing good sentences. This technical side is called **mechanics**. Using proper mechanics helps other people to understand what you write. Mechanics includes what you already learned about correct sentence structure. It also includes other details that make sentences correct. For now, we will look at some **punctuation** rules.

END MARKS

An **end mark** is placed at the end of a sentence. End marks are **periods, exclamation points, and question marks**.

Use a **period** to punctuate a statement (declarative sentence).

> The car zoomed around the track.

Use a **period** to punctuate a mild command (imperative sentence).

> Go to the corner, and turn right.

Use a **question mark** to punctuate a question (interrogative sentence).

> Will you please bring me some lemonade?

Use an **exclamation point** to end an exclamation (exclamatory sentence). This shows excitement.

> I won five thousand dollars!

Use an **exclamation point** to punctuate a strong command, such as a strong imperative.

> Get away from the curb!

APOSTROPHES

Another important punctuation mark is the **apostrophe**. The apostrophe is used to show **possession**. For example:

> Scott's car: The car belongs to Scott.
>
> Juanita's cat: The cat belongs to Juanita.

If you need to show possession for a noun that is plural and ends in *s*, add only the apostrophe.

> ladies' restroom
>
> cats' play area
>
> students' schedules

If you need to show possession for a plural noun that does not end in *s*, add an apostrophe and an *s*.

> geese's crossing
>
> men's golf
>
> women's soccer

The apostrophe is also used in contractions. A **contraction** is one word made from two or more words. The apostrophe stands in for the missing letters.

> **Examples:**
>
> I am = I'm
>
> you are = you're
>
> would not = wouldn't
>
> of the clock = o'clock

In formal writing, like an essay for class or for a test, you should not use too many contractions. They are considered informal language.

QUOTATION MARKS

Use **quotation marks** to show when someone is talking. The marks will enclose a direct quotation— someone's exact words. These marks also are used to show titles of stories, poems, songs, and other short works.

> "I want Cool Ranch Doritos," the girl said.
>
> The teacher spoke to her students saying, "You all have done such wonderful work today."
>
> Last night, I downloaded "Joy to the World" to my MP3 player.

For more about punctuation, review chapter 6.

Practice 5: Punctuation

ELA5C1.f

Look at each group of sentences. Decide which one has been written correctly.

1. A. "The cars are zooming by us," she said in amazement.
   B. "The cars' are zooming by us, she" said in amazement?
   C. "The cars are zooming by us, she said in amazement!
   D. "The car's are zooming by us she: said in amazement"

2. A. Where is the girls' locker room!
   B. Where is the girls locker room.
   C. Where is the girls's locker room?
   D. Where is the girls' locker room?

3. A. Please put my keys on the counter?
   B. Please put my keys' on the counter.
   C. Please put my keys on the counter.
   D. Please put my key's on the counter?

4. A. Will you go to the store with me.
   B. Will you go to the store with me?
   C. "Will you go' to the store with me!
   D. "Will you go to the store with me?

5. A. After the movie we can have ice cream.
   B. After the movie. We can have ice cream.
   C. After the movie, we can have ice cream.
   D. After the movie; we can have ice cream.

CHAPTER 2 SUMMARY

A **declarative sentence** makes a statement. It tells something.

An **interrogative sentence** asks a question. It ends in a question mark.

An **imperative sentence** gives a command. It makes a request or asks to have something done.

An **exclamatory sentence** shows excitement. It is punctuated with an exclamation mark.

A **clause** is a group of words that contains a verb and its subject. It is used as a part of a sentence. There are two kinds of clauses. An **independent clause** expresses a complete thought. It can stand alone as a sentence. A **dependent clause** cannot stand alone as a sentence.

A **simple sentence** has one independent clause and no dependent clauses.

A **compound sentence** is formed when two or more simple sentences are joined together.

A **complex sentence** has one independent clause plus one or more dependent clauses.

A **compound-complex sentence** has two or more independent clauses and at least one dependent clause.

A **fragment** is a group of words that is punctuated like a sentence but lacks a subject, predicate, or both.

Run-ons occur when a writer joins two or more complete sentences without using proper punctuation or conjunctions.

An **end mark** is a punctuation placed at the end of a sentence. End marks are **periods, exclamation points**, and **question marks**.

Another important punctuation mark is the **apostrophe**. The apostrophe is used to show **possession** and **contraction**.

Use **quotation marks** to indicate when someone speaks or the title of a short work.

CHAPTER 2 REVIEW

ELA5C1.e, f

For questions 1 through 6, identify the kind of sentence.

1. My favorite television show airs on Saturday morning.

   A. declarative

   B. interrogative

   C. imperative

   D. exclamatory

2. There is a burglar in the kitchen!

   A. declarative

   B. interrogative

   C. imperative

   D. exclamatory

3. Will you please leave me alone?

   A. declarative

   B. interrogative

   C. imperative

   D. exclamatory

4. Go to the freezer, and get me some vanilla ice cream.

   A. declarative

   B. interrogative

   C. imperative

   D. exclamatory

5. Will you please stop snoring?

   A. declarative

   B. interrogative

   C. imperative

   D. exclamatory

6. Watch carefully for the light to turn green.
   - A. declarative
   - B. interrogative
   - C. imperative
   - D. exclamatory

For questions 7 through 12, identify the sentence type.

7. I will not finish right now.
   - A. simple
   - B. compound
   - C. complex
   - D. compound-complex

8. Since Gertrude had started school, her mother had found time to catch up on reading.
   - A. simple
   - B. compound
   - C. complex
   - D. compound-complex

9. I like to play computer games, and I do not like to study.
   - A. simple
   - B. compound
   - C. complex
   - D. compound-complex

10. When the bell rings, we know it is the end of the day, so we are eager to get home.
   - A. simple
   - B. compound
   - C. complex
   - D. compound-complex

11. I like to play outside with my friends.

    A. simple

    B. compound

    C. complex

    D. compound-complex

12. The creature lives in the lake, and it only comes out at night.

    A. simple

    B. compound

    C. complex

    D. compound-complex

For questions 13 through 18, choose the sentence that uses correct punctuation AND grammar.

13. A. Misty said, I am very tired?

    B. Misty said, "I am very tired?"

    C. Misty said I am very tired!

    D. Misty said, "I am very tired."

14. A. When will I be old enough to drive?

    B. When will I be old enough to drive'

    C. "When will I" be old enough to drive?

    D. When will I be old' enough to drive?"

15. A. I will brush my teeth and then, I will take nap.

    B. I will brush my teeth, and then I will take a nap.

    C. I will brush my teeth and, then I will take a nap.

    D. none of these

16. A. Stephanie's best friend is Wallace.

    B. Stephanies best friend is Wallace.

    C. Stephani'es best friend is Wallace

    D. none of these

17. A. The hall monitor watch the boy run down the hall.

    B. The hall monitor watching the boy run down the hall.

    C. The hall monitor watched the boy run down the hall.

    D. none of these

18. A. My mother said, she will attend the school concert.

    B. My mother said she will attend, the school concert.

    C. My mother said she will attend the school concert.

    D. none of these

For questions 19 through 22, decide if the underlined part of the sentence is an independent clause or a dependent clause.

19. <u>If he chases me</u>, I will shout and run away.

    A. independent clause

    B. dependent clause

20. <u>The pizza could have been cheesier</u>, but I like it.

    A. independent clause

    B. dependent clause

21. Since last year, <u>I have become a really good volleyball player</u>.

    A. independent clause

    B. dependent clause

22. Did you understand <u>what she said</u>?

    A. independent clause

    B. dependent clause

Chapter 3
Planning the Essay

This chapter addresses the Grade 5 Writing Assessment rubric and covers the following GPS standard::

ELA5W1 The student produces writing that establishes an appropriate organizational structure, sets a context and engages the reader, maintains a coherent focus throughout, and signals a satisfying closure. The student

a. Selects a focus, an organizational structure, and a point of view based on purpose, genre expectations, audience, length, and format requirements.

Do you know how to swim? If you don't, think about someone saying, "Swim across that pool." It might seem impossible. However, when you break down the process of learning to swim into steps, it is easier. The first step is to get in the water. The next step might be waving your arms and legs in the water to stay afloat. Then, someone needs to show you how to move your arms and legs properly to propel through the water. Finally, you can perfect your style to move even faster. That was easy, wasn't it? You just took the first steps in learning to swim.

Like learning to swim, learning to write can be broken down into steps—the steps of writing are called the **writing process**. As you complete each step of the process, you are closer to a finished essay. The first step is **planning**.

In this chapter, you will see how a student named Sam follows the steps of the writing process. Through these steps, he will build his essay. In the next few chapters, you will see additional steps as he works on his essay.

Here is Sam's writing prompt:

Think about a time when you were proud of yourself. What happened, and what did you do that made you proud? Write a story about it that will appear in the school paper.

GETTING STARTED

How do you start the writing process? Once you know the question, the first step is to start thinking of ideas and writing them down on paper. This is called **prewriting**—anything you do before actually starting your draft.

BRAINSTORMING

One way to get started is to **brainstorm**. When you brainstorm you spend a few minutes writing down everything you can think of about a topic. Even if it sounds silly, write it down anyway. Write everything that comes to mind, even if you don't think you will use it. Later, you will decide which ideas to use.

Sam's Essay

Brainstorming List

sports

basketball

swimming

spelling bee—2nd place

first "A" in math

that some kids were picking on my friend and I stopped them

learning to ride a bike

DECIDING ON THE ESSAY TOPIC

Once you have some ideas on paper, it is time to decide which of your ideas you will write about. The next step is to choose an idea and a focus.

Of the things you have written on your paper, which is the best to use for your essay? You can ask yourself some questions to narrow down your ideas.

Questions to ask:

Does the idea answer the question?

Do I know enough about this idea to write an essay about it?

Do I have enough examples?

Sam asks himself the questions on page 36. He reads his brainstorming list. Then, he starts to narrow down his ideas.

- He crosses out "sports" because that topic is too broad.

- He crosses out "basketball" and "swimming." He likes both but can't think of a specific time he was proud about either.

- He crosses out "spelling bee—2nd place." He did well but wanted first place.

- He crosses out "learning to ride a bike" because that was a long time ago and he does not remember it very well.

Sam looks at the two ideas left: "first A in math" and "that time kids were picking on my friend and I stopped them." He chooses "first A in math." He thinks that he has the most to say about this idea.

Writing Tip

Some writers keep a notebook of things they know about or are interested in. You can do this too. Write down words you like, animals you think are interesting, games you enjoy, people you admire, or favorite memories. Some people like to write their dreams or a funny conversation. Writers use bits from real life in their writing. By writing down these items, you can remember them and use them when you need to.

CHOOSING A FOCUS

Now, it is time to choose a **focus** for your idea. To choose the focus, you will need to know the **purpose** of the essay. The purpose might be to persuade, to inform, or to entertain. Purpose differs depending on the question. It is important to identify the kind of essay you are being asked to write.

There are three different kinds of essays you might be asked to write. These types are **narrative**, **informational**, and **persuasive**. These three different types, or **genres**, have different purposes. Read on to learn more about these three types of essays. You will learn more about each of these genres in chapters 7, 8, and 9.

NARRATIVE

Narrative writing tells a story. The story can come from the writer's experience or imagination.

Example of a narrative writing prompt:

> Tell about something that happened during your summer vacation.

INFORMATIONAL

Informational writing helps the reader understand something. The writer might instruct, explain, or describe a thing or an idea.

Example of an informational writing prompt:

> Describe how to play your favorite board game.

PERSUASIVE

Persuasive writing tries to convince the reader to change his ideas or to take action.

Example of a persuasive writing prompt:

> What is the best way for kids to make a difference in the world?

It is important to know the purpose and the genre when choosing your focus. For example, pretend that your writing prompt is the informational one above. Your task is to describe how to play a game. Now, pretend that you write about the time you and your friend stayed up all night playing Monopoly. While you are talking about a board game, you are not answering the question. Be sure that both your topic <u>and</u> your focus answer the question asked.

Practice 1: Writing Process

ELA5W1.a

Read the information below. Then, answer the questions that follow.

You have been given the following writing prompt:

> Describe how to make a sandwich.

1. What kind of essay should you write for this prompt?

    A. narrative

    B. informational

    C. persuasive

    D. genre

2. Which would be the best focus for this essay?

    A. the steps to making a sandwich

    B. your favorite kind of sandwich

    C. where you like to eat lunch

    D. how the sandwich tastes

You have been given the following writing prompt:

> What is the best invention of all time? Explain why you think so.

3. What kind of essay should you write for this prompt?

    A. narrative

    B. informational

    C. persuasive

    D. genre

4. Which would be the best focus for this essay?

    A. a list of inventions

    B. a discussion of the two greatest inventors

    C. a list of gadgets that break easily

    D. a discussion of why your choice is best

5. Read Sam's writing prompt again. Brainstorm your own list of ideas. Choose an idea and a focus. Explain to a classmate why you chose as you did.

Sam's writing prompt:

> Think about a time when you were proud of yourself. What happened, and what did you do that made you proud? Write a story that will appear in the school paper.

6. Create brainstorming lists for one or more of the following topics:
   - importance of family
   - times you were scared
   - how to study
   - advantages/disadvantages (choose one) of a certain job
   - a fantasy vacation
   - compare/contrast two movies
   - the last time you cried
   - how to plant a garden

CHOOSING HOW TO ORGANIZE

Once you have your idea, it is time to think about how to organize your essay. Good **organization** helps the reader to understand your point. Organizing is part of the prewriting step in the writing process. When you organize, you think about how your ideas will fit together. There are several things you can do to organize your ideas.

THINK ABOUT THE GENRE

Narrative essays often tell a story in the order that it happened (chronologically).

Informational essays often describe a process step by step (sequentially).

Persuasive essays often argue point by point.

THINK ABOUT YOUR AUDIENCE

Who is your reader? Some readers will need more information about your topic than others will. Do you need to spend a section describing part of your topic? Or, would most people reading your essay already know this?

USE A GRAPHIC ORGANIZER

As you think about organizing your essay, it can be helpful to see how your ideas fit together. A **graphic organizer** is a way to see your ideas on paper.

One type of graphic organizer is a **cluster**.

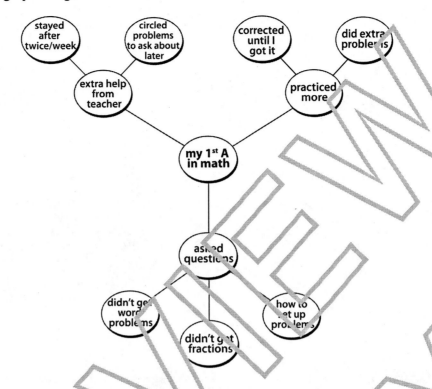

When you cluster, you write the main idea in the middle. Sam wrote, "my 1st A in math." Supporting ideas come next. Sam wrote, "asked questions," "extra help from teacher," and "practiced more." Finally, the examples or details branch off the supporting ideas. Sam wrote "didn't get fractions, didn't get word problems, how to set up problems," "stayed after twice/week, circled problems to ask about later," and "did extra problems, corrected until I got it."

Clustering shows you how the parts of your essay fit together. You can see if you have enough support for the main idea. You see if the main idea is too general or too specific. Clustering helps you organize your thoughts. You can see the different parts of the essay and determine what goes together.

There are many kinds of graphic organizers. Some are specific to the kind of essay.

A **Venn diagram** is two overlapping circles (see the next page). It shows similarities and differences of two items. On the overlapping part of the circles, write the similarities. In the other parts, write the differences. For example, if your topic is cats and dogs, one circle would be for dogs and the other for cats. A difference might be that dogs bark, while cats meow. A similarity would be that they both are common pets. You might use a Venn diagram if your topic asks you to compare and contrast.

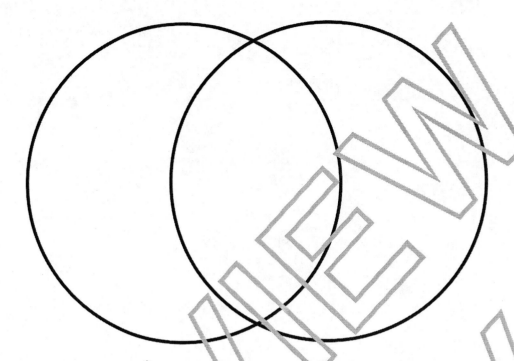

A **fishbone map** shows cause and effect. It provides spaces for you to list the cause, effect, and details of an event.

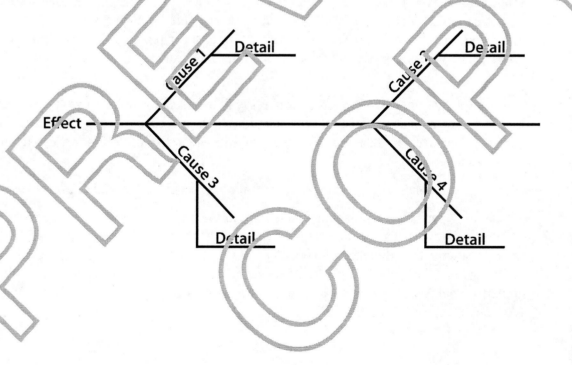

Practice 2: Organization

ELA5W1.a

Read the information below. Then, answer the questions that follow.

1. Which type of graphic organizer is best for this prompt?

   > Discuss the similarities and differences between frogs and turtles.

   A. fishbone map   C. clustering

   B. Venn diagram   D. prewriting

2. Which type of graphic organizer is best for this prompt?

   > Explain the effects of smoking.

   A. fishbone map   C. clustering

   B. Venn diagram   D. prewriting

Read the cluster map below. Then, answer the questions that follow.

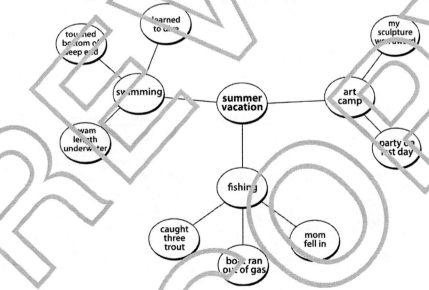

3. What is the main idea?
   A. learned to dive   C. art camp

   B. fishing   D. summer vacation

4. Which of the following are examples?
   A. swimming, fishing   C. summer vacation, art camp

   B. Mom fell in, learned to dive   D. caught three trout, fishing

REQUIREMENTS FOR THE TEST ESSAY

When you take the Georgia Grade 5 Writing Assessment, you will want to focus on several important aspects. As you plan your essay, think about the finished product. When your essay is graded, your score will depend on how well you do the following:

IDEAS

- How well did you show the main idea of the essay?
- Did you stay focused on the idea throughout the essay?
- Did you use examples, details, and facts to support your idea?

> **Example:** In his essay, Sam's main point will be to show how he earned an A in math. All of his examples will show how he worked to do this.

ORGANIZATION

- How well did you organize your ideas?
- Does the order of your ideas make sense for the prompt given?

> **Example:** In his essay, Sam will show how everything he did worked together to help him earn an A.

STYLE

- How well do you use language? For instance, do you use interesting words to keep the reader's interest?

> **Example:** In his essay, Sam will use different kinds of sentences for variety. He will use words that make the essay interesting. Descriptions and dialogue can help him tell his story.

CONVENTIONS

Do you use complete, correct sentences?

Are your grammar and spelling correct?

> **Example:** Sam will check his essay for correct spelling. He will make sure that he has written in complete sentences. He will proofread his essay to make sure his grammar and punctuation are correct.

Think about these requirements as you plan your essay. They will help you write a stronger essay. For more about these domains, review chapter 10.

Practice 3: Essay Requirements

ELA5W1.a

Read the paragraph below. Think about the requirements for the test essay. Then, answer the questions.

People should wear helmets every time they ride there bikes. Bike accidents are common. Head injuries from bike falls are common. A head injury is very serious. A helmet protects a person's head in case of a fall. When my cousin fell off her bike last year, she was not wearing a helmet. She got a concussion. The doctor said that she would not have gotten one if she'd had a helmet.

1. Which of the following best describes the main idea of this paragraph?
   A. my cousin's head injury
   B. how to ride a bike
   C. how doctors help bikers
   D. bike helmets keep you safe

2. Which of these sentences would be the best way to end this paragraph?
   A. I wouldn't want to be a doctor.
   B. I don't like riding bikes anymore.
   C. Helmets are important to keep bikers safe.
   D. She also sprained her wrist.

   Bike accidents are common. Head injuries from bike falls are common.

3. What is the best way to combine the two sentences without changing the meaning?
   A. Bike accidents are common, and falls often result in serious head injuries.
   B. Bike accidents are common and so are falls and head injuries.
   C. Bike accidents and head injuries are commonly serious.
   D. Bike accidents are common, falls are serious.

Reread the first sentence of the paragraph:

People should wear helmets every time they ride there bikes.

4. Which word is misspelled in the first sentence?
   A. change *there* to *their*
   B. change *wear* to *ware*
   C. change *bikes* to *bike's*
   D. change *helmets* to *helmetes*

CHAPTER 3 SUMMARY

Like anything that has several steps, **writing is a process**.

Brainstorming helps you get your ideas on paper.

Once you choose an idea, choose a **focus** that will best answer the question. Your essay could be **narrative**, **informational**, or **persuasive**.

When you **organize** your essay, think about your **purpose** and your **audience**. Use a **graphic organizer** to help see your ideas on paper.

Remember the big picture as you plan your essay. Your essay will be graded on **ideas**, **organization**, **style**, and **conventions**.

CHAPTER 3 REVIEW

ELA5W1.a

Read the information below. Then, answer the questions.

You have been given the following writing prompt:

> Describe a frightening dream you've had.

1. What kind of essay should you write for this prompt?
   - A. narrative
   - B. informational
   - C. persuasive
   - D. genre

You have been given the following writing prompt:

> What one book should every fifth grader read? Why?

2. What kind of essay should you write for this prompt?
   - A. narrative
   - B. informational
   - C. persuasive
   - D. genre

3. Which type of graphic organizer is best for the following prompt?

> Have you seen a movie version of a book you have read? Compare and contrast the book and the movie.

A. fishbone map

B. Venn diagram

C. clustering

D. prewriting

4. Which type of graphic organizer is best for the following prompt?

> Have you ever been late? Describe what happened to make you late. What happened after you were late?

A. fishbone map

B. Venn diagram

C. clustering

D. prewriting

Read the paragraph below. Then, answer the questions.

_____. Before 911, the police, ambulance, and fire station all had different phone numbers. In an emergency, some people had trouble finding these phone numbers. Some people memorized the numbers but could not recall them during an emergency. An emergency require fast action. With 911, people can save time by dialing a single, easy number.

5. Which of the following best describes the main idea of this paragraph?

A. the importance of the 911 phone system

B. different kinds of emergencies

C. how to call 911

D. why to call 911

6. Which of these sentences would best fill in the blank at the beginning of the paragraph?

A. I had to call 911 once when I was 7 years old.

B. There are some problems with the 911 system.

C. The 911 phone system is important to every community.

D. Before phones, how did people get emergency help?

Reread the second sentence:

> Before 911, the police, ambulance, and fire station all had different phone numbers.

7. Which of the following words is misspelled in this sentence?
   A. police
   B. ambulance
   C. different
   D. there are no errors

Reread the fifth sentence:

> An emergency require fast action.

8. Which version is correct?
   A. An emergencies requires fast action.
   B. An emergency requires fast action.
   C. A emergency require fast action.
   D. there are no errors

9. Make a brainstorming list for the following writing prompt:

If you could have one career, what would it be?

10. Use the following writing prompt to create a clustering graphic organizer:

What is your favorite food? Why?

11. Use the following information to make a Venn diagram:

Soccer	Basketball
team sport	5 players
11 players	timed game
requires coordination	play on court
play on field	team sport
fouls	need stamina to play
have a goalie	no goalie
cannot use hands (except goalie)	uses hands, not feet
penalty shots	penalty shots
timed game	fouls

Chapter 4
Drafting the Essay

This chapter addresses the Grade 5 Writing Assessment Ideas, Organization, and Style rubrics and covers the following GPS standards:

> **ELA5W1 The student produces writing that establishes an appropriate organizational structure, sets a context and engages the reader, maintains a coherent focus throughout, and signals a satisfying closure. The student**
>
> b. Writes texts of a length appropriate to address the topic or tell the story.
>
> c. Uses traditional structures for conveying information (e.g., chronological order, cause and effect, similarity and difference, and posing and answering a question).

Have you ever used a map? If you have, then you know it is helpful to have a guide to help you find your way. You can use guides when you write too. Following a certain format helps to build a strong essay.

FIVE-PARAGRAPH ESSAY

When you are asked to write an essay, you will often be expected to write a **five-paragraph essay**. A five-paragraph essay follows a specific format. Each paragraph has its own purpose. Use the guide in this chapter to keep your writing on track.

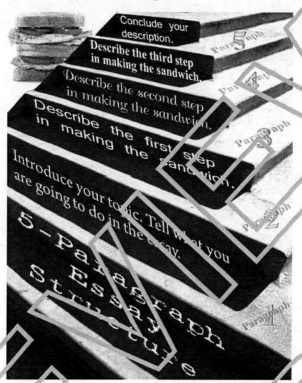

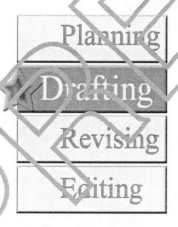

Now, you have thought about the writing topic and done some prewriting. The next step of the writing process is **drafting**. When you draft your essay, you further organize your ideas from prewriting. During this step, the main goal is to get your thoughts on paper in a logical order. Spelling and grammar don't matter in the drafting stage. These steps will come later.

Watch as Sam builds his essay using the five-paragraph essay guide. Since this is Sam's draft, you will see all kinds of errors. Sam will work on these in the next steps of the writing process.

Do you remember Sam's writing prompt? Here it is again:

Think about a time when you were proud of yourself. What happened, and what did you do that made you proud? Write a story that will appear in the school paper.

FIRST PARAGRAPH

The first paragraph is the **introduction**. In the first sentence, begin with some background information to introduce your idea. As you tell more about your idea in the next sentence or two, be more specific. An important sentence in the introduction is the thesis statement. The **thesis statement** tells the point you will make in the essay

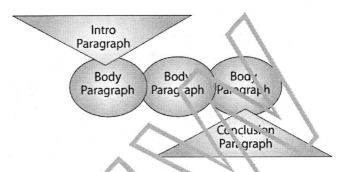

and the three main ways you will make that point. In this way, it acts as an outline for your body paragraphs.

Here is the structure of the first paragraph:

- background
- thesis statement

SECOND, THIRD, AND FOURTH PARAGRAPHS

Each main point from the thesis sentence gets its own paragraph. The second, third, and fourth paragraphs all follow the same structure. There is one main point per paragraph. The main points are in the same order that you listed them in your thesis statement. This part of the essay is called the **body** of the essay.

In the first sentence of each paragraph, **state the point** you will make in that paragraph. In the next few sentences, provide **proof** for your point. Proof might be an example, a quote, or a statistic. Then, **explain** how the proof supports your point. This explanation is also called the **analysis**.

Here is the structure for the second, third, and fourth paragraphs:

- statement
- proof
- analysis

FIFTH PARAGRAPH

The fifth paragraph is the **conclusion** paragraph. You can think of the fifth paragraph as a reverse of the first paragraph. Don't just copy your first paragraph, though. It is important to write your thoughts in an original way for the conclusion. The conclusion is the last thing your reader sees, and it is your last chance to make an impression. Restate your main points, restate your thesis, then leave the reader with a compelling thought or question.

Here is the structure of the fifth paragraph:

- thesis statement
- final thought

Here is Sam's draft, based on this five-paragraph guide:

Since first grade, I have always earn C's in Math. I got a 72 in first grade, I think a 78 in second grade, a 77 in third grade, and a 75 in fourth grade. This year, I was very proud to earn my first A in math. My A came from a lot of hard work and I got it by asking questions, getting extra help from my teacher, and practice.

The first step I took toward earning an A was to ask questions. Before, I was quite during math, hoping my teacher would not notice me. This year, I decided to ask questions about everything under the sun including the things I don't get—fractions and word problems. It worked! When I asked questions in class, my teacher explained until I got it.

I asked my teacher for extra help. I stayed after school twice a week. Some other kids were there sometimes too. Then, my teacher showed me now to apply what we did in class to the homework. I also circled problems from the class work that I didn't get. My teacher explain it all until it made sense.

I practiced more. My teacher gave me extra homework problems so I practice until fractions and word problems was easy! I was really tired from all of that extra work. I know what your thinking—who wants more homework? But for me, practice made perfect. I also went back and corrected anything I got wrong from the class work or the homework. All of that practice paid off.

By practicing, getting extra help, and asking questions, I got a A. I worked hard this year, and I am very proud of myself. I learned something besides fractions too. I learned that if I decide to be good at something, I can do it.

The length of your five-paragraph essay will depend on the prompt and your topic. On the Grade 5 Writing Assessment, you will not need to write an essay of specific length. However, think about the structure of a five-paragraph essay. A paragraph is generally three to five sentences long. Also consider what you need to write to end up with a well-developed essay.

Practice 1: Five-Paragraph Essay

ELA5W1.b

Read the information below. Then, answer the questions.

Reread Sam's introduction.

Since first grade, I have always earn C's in Math. I got a 72 in first grade, I think a 78 in second grade, a 77 in third grade, and a 75 in fourth grade. This year, I was very proud to earn my first A in math. My A came from a lot of hard work and I got it by asking questions, getting extra help from my teacher, and practice.

1. Which is the thesis statement?

   A. Since first grade, I have always earn C's in Math.

   B. My A came from a lot of hard work and I got it by asking questions, getting extra help from my teacher, and practice

   C. I got a 72 in first grade, I think a 78 in second grade, a 77 in third grade, and a 75 in fourth grade.

   D. none of the above

2. Which general statement is Sam using to introduce his topic?

   A. My A came from a lot of hard work and I got it by asking questions, getting extra help from my teacher, and practice.

   B. This year, I was very proud to earn my first A in math.

   C. Since first grade, I have always earn C's in Math.

   D. none of the above

Reread Sam's fourth paragraph.

I practiced more. My teacher gave me extra homework problems so I practice until fractions and word problems was easy! I was really tired from all of that extra work. I know what your thinking— who wants more homework? But for me, practice made perfect. I also went back and corrected anything I got wrong from the class work or the homework. All of that practice paid off.

3. Which sentence states the point Sam will make in this paragraph?

   A. All of that practice paid off.

   B. I also went back and corrected anything I got wrong from the class work or the homework.

   C. I practiced more.

   D. But for me, practice made perfect.

4. What proof does Sam give in this paragraph?

   A. My teacher gave me extra homework problems so I practice until fractions and word problems was easy!

   B. I practiced more.

   C. I know what your thinking—who wants more homework?

   D. All of that practice paid off.

5. Taking your notes from any of the prewriting topics you wrote about in chapter 3, compose a five-paragraph essay. Use Sam's essay as a model.

ORGANIZING

In chapter 3, you read about using graphic organizers. Those helped to organize your thoughts.

Now, think about organizing ideas into the paragraphs of an essay. The order of ideas will depend on the type of essay you are writing. Here are some common **organizational patterns**. We will discuss the way each can be used to order an essay.

CHRONOLOGICAL ORDER

One way to organize an essay is chronologically. **Chronological order** tells events in order, from first to last. You can think of chronological order as a series of events or steps. This makes chronological order a good pattern for narrative or informational essays.

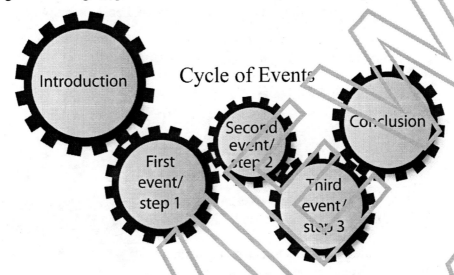

Remember to also follow the five-paragraph essay structure. When organizing an essay chronologically, here is how the structure would look:

Paragraph 1: Introduction

Paragraph 2: First event or step

Paragraph 3: Second event or step

Paragraph 4: Third event or step

Paragraph 5: Conclusion

Example: You are answering the writing prompt, "Describe how to make a pizza." You are describing a process. The best way to describe this process is to show the steps in order.

Paragraph 1: Introduce your topic. Tell what you are going to do in the essay.

Paragraph 2: Describe the first step in making the pizza.

Paragraph 3: Describe the second step in making the pizza.

Paragraph 4: Describe the third step in making the pizza.

Paragraph 5: Conclude your description.

Narrative essays are usually organized chronologically. The writer tells a story in the order it happened. We read the first event, the second event, and the final outcome.

Informational essays can also be organized chronologically. A writer explains a process in step-by-step detail. We read what to do first, second, third, and so on.

Practice 2: Organizing Chronologically

ELA5W1.c

Read the information below. Then, answer the questions.

1. The sentences in this paragraph are out of order. Choose the correct order.

    > 1) Then, I leave a glass on water on the counter to drink as soon as I get home. 2)When I get ready to go running, I have certain things I always do. 3) Next, I put on my sneakers. 4) First, I put on my running clothes. 5) Finally, I take off.

    A. 1, 2, 3, 4, 5

    B. 5, 4, 3, 2, 1

    C. 2, 4, 3, 1, 5

    D. 4, 2, 3, 1, 5

Pretend that you are writing a five-paragraph essay describing how to make a bed.

2. Write the following ideas in chronological order on the lines below.

    Introduction, Conclusion, Put on sheets, Arrange pillows, Put on blankets

    A. Paragraph 1: _____

    B. Paragraph 2: _____

    C. Paragraph 3: _____

    D. Paragraph 4: _____

    E. Paragraph 5: _____

3. Write a five-paragraph essay for the following prompt. Use chronological order.

    > Imagine you wake up to find yourself on a new planet, one you've never seen before. There is a note by your bed saying you have one day to enjoy this new planet. Write a story about how you would spend that one day.

CAUSE AND EFFECT

An essay that is organized with **cause and effect** shows the relationship between events. As with chronological organization, the order of events is important. When organizing an essay using cause and effect, your focus is the **relationship** between the events.

In chapter 3, you saw how to use a fishbone map to organize your thoughts during prewriting. Now, see how you can use it to organize cause and effect.

Read the fishbone map below. It shows the effect of Ellie's forgetfulness.

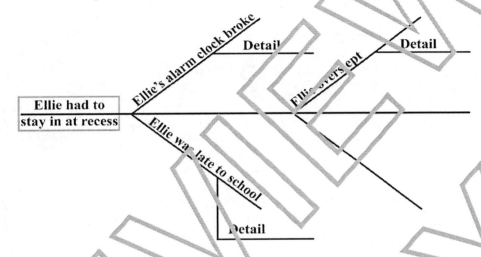

Cause 1: Ellie's alarm clock broke.

Cause 2: Ellie overslept.

Cause 3: Ellie was late for school.

Effect: Ellie had to stay in at recess to finish work she missed in the morning.

You can think of cause and effect like a chain of events.

To find out a cause, ask, "Why did this happen?"

To find out an effect, ask, "What happened because of this?"

Cause and effect organization follows the five-paragraph essay structure. Persuasive essays can be organized using cause and effect. When using this structure, the writer shows how one event led to another.

Practice 3:   Organizing with Cause and Effect

ELA5W1.c

Label each sentence C if it is a cause. Label it E if it is an effect.

1.   John forgot his umbrella. ___ John got wet. ___

2.   Viktor won the swim meet. ___ Viktor practiced hard. ___

3.   Kate studied for her test. ___ Kate got an A. ___

4.   Aiko raked leaves in her yard. ___ Aiko earned five dollars. ___

5.   Nellie got 2nd place. ____ Nellie practiced for the spelling bee. ___

6.   Most people have had an injury at some point in their lives. Think of a time you have gotten hurt. What happened?

Use a fishbone map to show the causes and the effect.

Use your map to fill in the paragraph guide below. Show how you would organize your ideas in an essay.

Paragraph 1: Introduction

Paragraph 2: _____

Paragraph 3: _____

Paragraph 4: _____

Paragraph 5: Conclusion

7.   Using your fishbone map, write a five-paragraph essay about a time when you got hurt.

SIMILARITIES AND DIFFERENCES

A writing prompt that asks you to discuss similarities and differences is asking you to **compare and contrast**. Think about the ways two things are alike and the ways they are different.

In chapter 3, you saw how to use a Venn diagram to organize your thoughts during prewriting. Now, see how you can use it to organize an essay using compare and contrast.

Read the Venn diagram below. It shows a comparison of birds and fish as pets.

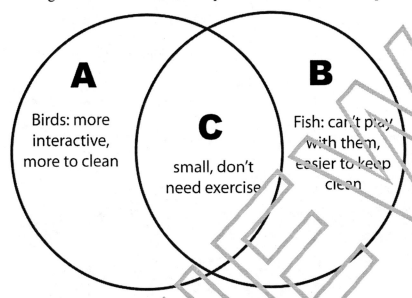

You can use the information in a Venn diagram to help organize your essay using compare and contrast. Now that you see how the two things are alike and different, think about the best way to organize these ideas into an essay. Your purpose is to show similarities and differences in these two pets.

A compare and contrast essay follows the five-paragraph essay structure. You have two options for organizing an essay using compare and contrast. The first is to organize it **one side at a time**.

Paragraph 1: Introduction

Paragraph 2: Describe birds and fish

Paragraph 3: Talk about birds and all their features as pets

Paragraph 4: Talk about fish and all their features as pets

Paragraph 5: Conclusion

The second option is to organize **point by point**.

Paragraph 1: Introduction

Paragraphs 2–4: Discuss the features of both types of pets point by point; divide paragraphs by topics such as how much you can play with each, the cleaning involved with each, their size, and so on.

Paragraph 5: Conclusion

Informational essays can be organized using compare and contrast. When using this structure, the writer informs the reader how two things are alike and different.

Practice 4:   Organizing with Similarities and Differences

ELA5W1.c

1. Fill in the Venn diagram with the following information.

    Things to compare: cakes, cookies

Similarities:

*   both are desserts, both are sweet, can be different flavors

Differences:

*   Cake: need a fork to eat it, bake in a pan, moist texture
*   Cookies: can eat with your hands, bake on a cookie sheet, dense texture

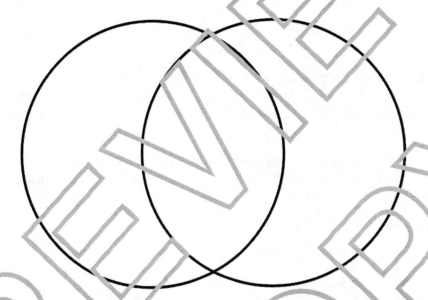

2. Now, use the Venn diagram to organize an essay using compare and contrast. Use the item by item method of organization. Fill in the blanks to organize the essay.

Paragraph 1: Introduction

Paragraph 2: _____

Paragraph 3–4: _____

Paragraph 5: Conclusion

3. Write a five-paragraph essay about cakes and cookies. You may use the Venn diagram. You can organize your essay item by item or feature by feature.

QUESTION AND ANSWER

An essay that uses a **question and answer** structure poses a question and then answers that question. This type of organization moves point by point.

When you write an essay using question and answer organization, you are writing to tell your reader something. Think about your audience. You will ask questions that the audience will want to know.

Examples: If your essay is about basketball, what rules should you write about? What happens if players break the rules? Do you need special equipment?

If your essay is about water pollution, how does water get polluted? Who is solving the problem? What can kids do about it?

When you begin to organize your essay, think about the most important issue, question, or piece of information the reader needs to know. Depending on your topic, your questions and the answers may follow a logical progression or a chronological progression. They may be in order from most important to least important.

Essays using the question and answer structure follow the five-paragraph essay format. When organizing an essay using question and answer, follow this structure:

Paragraph 1: Introduction

Paragraph 2: First question with answer

Paragraph 3: Second question with answer

Paragraph 4: Third question with answer

Paragraph 5: Conclusion

Informational essays can use a question and answer structure. When using this structure, the writer informs the reader about important points of the topic.

Persuasive essays can also use a question and answer structure. When using this structure, the writer might try to show readers how their action is needed to solve a problem.

Practice 5: Organizing with Question and Answer

ELA5W1.c

Read the information below. Then answer the questions.

You are writing a letter to ask your principal to make field hockey a school sport. The questions you will answer in the essay are:

- Who will coach?
- Why should you make this a school sport?
- What equipment would we need?

1. Fill in the blanks below to organize the essay. Start with the most important question.

Paragraph 1: Introduction

Paragraph 2: _____

Paragraph 3: _____

Paragraph 4: _____

Paragraph 5: Conclusion

2. With a classmate, brainstorm a list of possible questions for the topic below.

   Topic: ways to improve recess at our school

   Audience: principal and teachers

3. Using the brainstorming list for the topic above, write a five-paragraph essay. Use the question-and-answer pattern.

CHAPTER 4 SUMMARY

In this chapter, you learned the format of the **five-paragraph essay**.

- Paragraph 1 is the **introduction** paragraph. Here, you state the point you will make in the essay.
- Paragraphs 2–4 are the **body** of the essay. Here, you discuss each point and show how each relates to your main point.
- Paragraph 5 is the **conclusion** paragraph. Here, you summarize your ideas in a way that leaves the reader thinking or ready to act.

You learned how to apply this structure to some common types of essays.

Chronological essays tell events in the order they occurred.

Cause and Effect essays show the relationship between events.

Similarity and Difference essays discuss the ways two things are alike and different.

Question and Answer essays pose a question then answer that question.

CHAPTER 4 REVIEW

ELA5W1.b, c

Reread Sam's second paragraph. Then, answer the questions that follow.

> *The first step I took toward erning an A was to ask questions. Before, I was quite during math, hoping my teacher would not notice me. This year I decided to ask questions about everything under the sun including the things I don't get—fractions and word problems. It worked! When I asked questions in class, my teacher explained until I got it.*

1. Which sentence states the **point** Sam will make in this paragraph?

    A. Before, I was quite during math, hoping my teacher would not notice me.

    B. It worked!

    C. The first step I took toward erning an A was to ask questions.

    D. When I asked questions in class, my teacher explained until I got it.

2. Which sentence states the **proof** Sam uses in this paragraph?

    A. This year, I decided to ask questions about…the things I don't get—fractions and word problems.

    B. The first step I took toward erning an A was to ask questions.

    C. When I asked questions in class, my teacher explained until I got it.

    D. Before, I was quite during math, hoping my teacher would not notice me.

3. Which sentence states the **analysis** Sam uses in this paragraph?

    A. This year, I decided to ask questions about the things I don't get—fractions and word problems.

    B. The first step I took toward erning an A was to ask questions.

    C. Before, I was quite during math, hoping my teacher would not notice me.

    D. When I asked questions in class, my teacher explained until I got it.

4. Matt is writing an essay. He is organizing his essay chronologically. His topic is how to grow a flower from a seed. Which shows the correct order of the main points in his essay?

    A. tend the seed, plant the seed, care for the flower

    B. plant the seed, tend the seed, care for the flower

    C. care for the flower, tend the seed, plant the seed

    D. plant the seed, care for the flower, tend the seed

5. Juan is writing an essay showing how skateboards and scooters are alike and different. How should he organize his essay?

    A. chronologically

    B. cause and effect

    C. similarity and difference

    D. question and answer

6. William is writing a question and answer essay. His audience is his principal. His topic is how to improve the school lunch menu. Which questions will the principal most likely have?

    A. how much these changes will cost, will the food be nutritious

    B. will the food taste good, can we eat outside

    C. who will cook the food, can we eat with our hands

    D. can parents visit at lunch, can we use real silverware

Fill in the blanks below with causes and effects.

Causes	Effects
7. My bike was stolen.	_____
8. _____	I made the basketball team.
9. _____	I got soaking wet.
10. My dog barked.	_____
11. _____	

12. Using the following writing prompt, create a five-paragraph essay. Before writing a draft, come up with an organizational pattern. Use a graphic organizer to focus your ideas. Then, write your essay.

    Many people continue debating the issue of crime and violence in our society. Explain the steps you would take to reduce crime and violence.

Keep this essay for later. You will use it in the next few chapters!

Chapter 5
Revising the Essay

This chapter addresses the Grade 5 Writing Assessment Ideas, Organization, and Style rubrics and covers the following GPS standards:

> **ELA5W1 The student produces writing that establishes an appropriate organizational structure, sets a context and engages the reader, maintains a coherent focus throughout, and signals a satisfying closure. The student**
>
> d. Uses appropriate structures to ensure coherence (e.g., transition elements).

When you try something new, do you get it right the first time? Most people don't. Writers don't either. They go back over what they've written, looking for ways to improve it. Every writer, from a new writer to a best-selling novelist, does this. This process is called **revising**, and it is the next step in the writing process.

WHAT IS REVISING?

When you revise, you improve your essay. You reread your essay and make changes. You may add or remove material. You may rewrite some parts. You may move some sentences around. In other words, **revising** is making the "big changes." The small corrections, like spelling and punctuation, come in the next step of the writing process. (You'll practice editing in the next chapter.)

Planning

Drafting

Revising

Editing

COHERENCE

When you revise, the first step is to give your essay **coherence**. In a coherent essay, everything you've written makes sense. Your ideas flow in a logical way. You stick to the point. Every sentence belongs, and every paragraph contributes to the main point you are making.

The first step is to reread your essay.

As you reread your essay, it is time to makes some changes. In chapters 7–9, you'll learn more about ways to revise specific types of essays. The checklists below give you some questions to ask about any essay. Use them to revise your essay and make it coherent.

Questions about organization

☐ Did I follow the structure for a five-paragraph essay?

☐ Did I follow the structure within each paragraph?

☐ Did I follow the order in my thesis statement?

☐ Did I state my main point in the first paragraph of paragraphs 2–4?

☐ Did I repeat any ideas?

☐ Did I keep all discussion on a particular topic in one place?

☐ Does everything belong where I put it?

☐ Do I need to add or delete anything?

Questions about main points, proof, and analysis

☐ Do my main points prove my thesis?

☐ Did I include good proof for each point?

☐ Did I explain how it all relates to the thesis?

Questions about effectiveness

☐ Did I answer the question in the writing prompt?

☐ Did I stick with my original purpose?

☐ Is my point clear?

☐ Did I stay on topic throughout the essay?

☐ Will the reader understand my ideas?

☐ Did I include irrelevant details?

☐ Do the sentences make sense together?

☐ Did I explain the relationship between my ideas?

☐ Does each sentence flow into the next?

☐ Are my introduction and conclusion effective?

Now, watch as Sam revises his essay. As Sam rereads his essay, he checks it for coherence. He begins with his introduction paragraph:

> *Since first grade, I have always earn C's in Math. I got a 72 in first grade, I think a 78 in second grade, a 77 in third grade and a 75 in fourth grade. This year, I was very proud to earn my first A in math. My A was from a lot of hard work and I got it by asking questions, getting extra help from my teacher, and practice.*

Sam decides to keep his first sentence. It gives some history and is a good way to introduce his topic.

Sam decides to delete his second sentence. His exact grades are small details that the reader does not need to know. This sentence does not help prove his point.

Sam decides to keep his third sentence. It tells what he was proud of, so it shows how his essay will address the prompt.

Sam changes some wording of his fourth sentence. He thinks that it makes the idea clearer to his reader.

Here is what the paragraph looks like after Sam revises it:

> *Since first grade, I have always earn C's in Math. This year, I was very proud to earn my first A in math. My A came as a result of a lot of hard work and I got it by asking questions, getting extra help from my teacher, and practice.*

Notice that the paragraph still contains some minor errors. Sam will work on these during the editing process. For now, Sam will work on his revisions using the coherence checklist. He will work paragraph by paragraph. Finally, he will check the coherence of the essay as a whole.

Writing Tip
All writers have to work at getting their words just right. Effective writing takes hard work and practice. Even famous authors revise their work. For example, Ernest Hemingway rewrote the conclusion to one of his books over thirty times before he was satisfied!

Practice 1: Coherence

ELA5W1.d

Read Sam's second paragraph. Then, answer the questions below.

1) The first step I took toward erning an A was to ask questions. 2) Before, I was quite during math, hoping my teacher would not notice me.
3) This year, I decided to ask questions about everything under the sun including the things I don't get—fractions and word problems. 4) It worked! 5) When I asked questions in class, my teacher explained until I got it.

1. Which sentence is casual and should be deleted if the essay audience changed from peers to the principal?

    A. sentence 1

    B. sentence 2

    C. sentence 3

    D. sentence 4

2. Which is the best way to revise sentence 3?

    A. This year, I decided to ask every single question about everything under the sun including the things I don't get –fractions and word problems.

    B. This year, I decided to ask questions about the things I don't understand—fractions and word problems.

    C. This year, I decided to ask some things.

    D. no change

3. Sentence 5 explains how asking questions helped Sam earn an A. Is this sentence in the right place?

    A. Yes.

    B. No. It should be the first sentence in the paragraph.

    C. No. It should be the second sentence in the paragraph.

    D. No. It should be the third sentence in the paragraph.

4. Short response: Should Sam delete sentence 2? Why or why not?

TRANSITIONS

Transitions help your writing to flow. Think of them as bridges. These bridges connect sentences, paragraphs, and ideas. They can also help the organization of an essay by showing order.

Effective transitions help the audience too. They improve coherence. Transitions can make your thought process easier for readers to follow.

Read the example below.

Without a transition: Toya loves cats. They make her sneeze.

With a transition: Toya loves cats <u>even though</u> they make her sneeze.

By adding a transition, the link between these two statements is clear.

There are many different transition words and phrases. They serve different purposes. The following lists show how to use transition words and phrases to accomplish different things.

Transition Types	
to show order of events or time	then, soon, finally
to show cause and effect	cause: because, since, due to
	effect: as a result, therefore, consequently
to compare and contrast	compare: like, in the same way, similarly
	contrast: but, rather, however
to give an example	for example, specifically, for instance

Now, watch as Sam revises his third paragraph to include transitions.

Here is Sam's third paragraph:

> *I asked my teacher for extra help. I stayed after school twice a week. Some other kids were there sometimes too. Then, my teacher showed me how to apply what we did in class to the homework I also circled problems from the class work that I didn't get. My teacher explain it all until it made sense.*

Sam thinks about his purpose in writing. He wants to show how the things he did resulted in an A in math. He decides to begin his second paragraph with a transition word to show that he is moving on to a new step.

Sam decides that it is important to show how staying after improved his grade. He realizes his sentence about other students does not move his point along, so he deletes it. He also adds a transition to his third sentence to shows what happened while he stayed after.

Here is what the paragraph looks like after Sam adds transitions:

> <u>Next,</u> I asked my teacher for extra help. I stayed after school twice a week. <u>During that time,</u> my teacher showed me how to apply what we did in class to the homework. I also circled problems from the class work that I didn't get. <u>Then,</u> my teacher explain it all until it made sense.

Of course, Sam will go through his entire essay to look for other places that may need transitions.

As you practice, keep a list of transitions handy. This will help you remember the transitions later, like when you take the Grade 5 Writing Assessment.

Writing Tip
Transition words are very important in many essays. Transition words help show the relationship between ideas and the sequence of events.

Practice 2: Transitions
ELA5W1.d

Choose the best transition word to fill in the blank.

1. I was tired after climbing the mountain, _____ I was proud of myself for making it all the way to the top!

   A. but

   B. then

   C. like

   D. soon

2. _____ lizards, starfish can re-grow missing body parts.

   A. Rather   B. Finally   C. Since   D. Like

3. _____ the bus broke down, we were late to school.

   A. Therefore   B. Because   C. For example   D. Consequently

4. Henry ate dinner, did the laundry, and washed the dishes. _____, his work was done, and he could go to sleep.

    A. Finally   B. Rather   C. However   D. Specifically

TONE AND VOICE

Another "big change" to look for is the overall **tone** of your essay. This is the attitude or feeling in your writing. By choosing the right words, you tell a reader what you are feeling.

Types of Tone	
angry	frustrated
apologetic	happy
calm	neutral
dramatic	rude
fearful	serious

The tone you use is also part of your writer's **voice**. Voice is the unique quality of your writing. The way that you use language in your essay will build your own writer's voice. It also means that your choice of words and phrasing is right for the topic and the audience. As you read over your draft, you want to make sure your voice is apparent throughout the essay.

In addition, by using *formal language*, you show that you know how to write a formal essay. For example, say that a prompt asked you to write a letter about after-school activities to the principle. You would not begin, "Hey, dude, I wanna talk about after-school stuff." You would say something more appropriate like, "Mr. Riley, I am writing to talk about after-school activities at our school." You should use formal language when you write your writing assessment essay.

Practice 3: Tone and Voice
ELA5W1

1. Think about writing a narrative about the best trip you ever took. What would be the best tone for this essay?

   A. tired   B. sad   C. worried   D. excited

2. To keep a consistent voice throughout the essay, you would make sure that

   A. you keep saying "I went" and "I did."

   B. all of the sentences were either short or long.

   C. the tone and formality were the same throughout.

   D. you first talked about what you liked, then what you didn't like

---

Writing Tip

Once you have written your essay, take a few minutes to go back and review the words you used. Have you used words accurately? Are some words repeated too many times? Do you need to use some synonyms? Can you eliminate some contractions? Can you add some adjectives to make the writing more interesting and descriptive?

CHAPTER 5 SUMMARY

When **revising** an essay, look for ways to make improvements.

Revise an essay to give it **coherence**. In a coherent essay, everything makes sense.

Transitions help an essay to be coherent. They show the relationships between ideas, helping your reader to follow your train of thought.

The **tone** of an essay is the attitude or feeling in the writing. **Voice** is the unique quality of your writing, created by how you use words and phrasing. Make sure tone and voice are consistent throughout the essay.

CHAPTER 5 REVIEW

ELA5W1.d

Help Sam revise the fourth paragraph of his essay. Read the paragraph, then answer the questions below.

> 1) _____ I practiced more. 2) My teacher gave me extra homework problems so I practice until fractions and word problems was easy! 3) I was reallytired from all of that extra work. 4) I know what your thinking—who wants more homework? 5) But for me, practice made perfect. 6) I also went back and corrected anything I got wrong from the class work or the homework. 7) All of that practice paid off.

1. Which transition would best fill in the blank in sentence 1?

    A. At first   B. Since   C. Finally   D. For example

2. Which sentence should be deleted because it does not relate to the main idea of the paragraph?

    A. sentence 1   B. sentence 3   C. sentence 6   D. sentence 7

Choose the best transitions to fill in the blanks.

3. ____, Cate measured the flour. ____, she added sugar.

    A. First, Then   C. Specifically, But

    B. Finally, Since   D. Like, Therefore

4. Giovanni went home early ____ his stomachache.

    A. soon   B. therefore   C. however   D. due to

5. Antoine keeps unusual pets. ____, last year he had a pet raccoon.

    A. Rather   B. For example   C. Finally   D. However

Read the paragraph below. Then, answer the questions.

> 1) My first time baking oatmeal cookies was a disaster! 2) I started out well, with the recipe and correct utensils laid out on the counter. 3) _____, I realized part way through the recipe that I did not have all of the ingredients. 4) In case you didn't know, salt is not a good substitute for sugar. 5) Though my cookies were horrible, I learned an important lesson about cooking—be prepared! 6) Cream of wheat does not do well in place of oatmeal, either.

6. Which two sentences should switch places for the best coherence?
   A. sentences 1 and 5
   B. sentences 5 and 6
   C. sentences 1 and 2
   D. sentences 5 and 6

7. Which transition best fills in the blank in sentence 3?
   A. Finally
   B. At last
   C. As a result of
   D. However

8. Which sentence should be deleted because it does not relate to the main idea?
   A. sentence 1
   B. sentence 3
   C. sentence 5
   D. none should be deleted

9. What tone is used in this paragraph?
   A. frustrated
   B. shocked
   C. cheerful
   D. frightened

10. Go back to the essay you wrote for question 12 in the chapter 4 review. Now revise it for coherence, transitions, tone, and voice. Here is the prompt again:

> Many people continue debating the issue of crime and violence in our society. Explain the steps you would take to reduce crime and violence.

Keep this revised draft for use in the next chapter!

Chapter 6
Editing the Essay

This chapter addresses the Grade 5 Writing Assessment Conventions rubric and covers the following GPS standard:

> **ELA5C1 The student demonstrates understanding and control of the rules of the English language, realizing that usage involves the appropriate application of conventions and grammar in both written and spoken formats. The student**
>
> f. Uses and identifies correct mechanics (e.g., apostrophes, quotation marks, comma use in compound sentences, paragraph indentations) and correct sentence structure (e.g., elimination of sentence fragments and run-ons).
>
> g. Uses additional knowledge of correct mechanics (e.g., apostrophes, quotation marks, comma use in compound sentences, paragraph indentations), correct sentence structure (e.g., elimination of fragments and run-ons), and correct Standard English spelling (e.g., commonly used homophones) when writing, revising, and editing.

In the previous three chapters, you reviewed the steps of the writing process. Step 1 was planning, in which you got some ideas on paper through brainstorming. You continued prewriting by organizing those ideas. Step 2 was drafting, in which you wrote the first draft of the essay. Step 3 was revising, in which you made the big improvements. This chapter covers the final step of the writing process: editing.

WHAT IS EDITING?

When you look for errors in your essay, you are **proofreading**. You are looking for small mistakes. Is everything spelled correctly? Are there commas in the correct places? Is each sentence complete? When you correct any errors you find, you are **editing**.

When you revised your essay, you asked yourself several questions to help that process. Here are some questions you can ask as you proofread your essay:

Planning

Drafting

Revising

⭐ Editing

Proofreading checklist

Sentences:
☐ Are all sentences complete?
☐ Did I use a variety of sentence lengths?

Punctuation:
☐ Did I use correct punctuation?

Verbs use:
☐ Does each verb agree with its subject?
☐ Is my verb tense consistent?

Spelling and capitalization:
☐ Is each word spelled correctly?
☐ Did I use correct capitalization?

Read on to learn how to effectively proofread your essay.

SENTENCE STRUCTURE

In chapter 2, you learned about complete sentences. Now, apply what you've learned to proofreading an essay.

As you proofread, read each sentence to be sure it is complete and correct. A sentence is a complete thought. Every sentence has a subject and a predicate.

FINDING AND FIXING SENTENCE FRAGMENTS

Remember, a **fragment** is an incomplete sentence. It can't stand alone.

To find sentence fragments, ask:

- Is it a complete thought?

- Does it have a subject and a predicate?

Incorrect: Xavier thought that the movie.

The example is not a complete thought. It leaves the reader asking, "What did Xavier think about the movie?"

Correct: Xavier thought that the movie was exciting.

FINDING AND FIXING RUN-ON SENTENCES

As you learned, a **run-on** is two complete sentences joined into one sentence with incorrect or no punctuation.

To find run-on sentences, look for independent clauses.

   Incorrect: Ben is a fast runner he is a natural athlete.

This is a run-on. It has two independent clauses: "Ben is a fast runner" and "he is a natural athlete." They are joined with no punctuation.

There are several ways to correct a run-on sentence.

1. Break it into two sentences.

   Correct: Ben is a fast runner. He is a natural athlete.

2. Join the independent clauses with a semicolon.
   Correct: Ben is a fast runner; he is a natural athlete.

3. Join the two independent clauses with a comma and a conjunction.
   Correct: Ben is a fast runner, for he is a natural athlete.

As you choose how to correct sentence fragments, think about the sentences you already have in your essay. Try to use a variety of sentence lengths. If you have already used many shorter sentences, choose a revision that corrects the run-on to one longer sentence.

For more about sentences, refer back to chapter 2.

Practice 1:   Sentence Structure

ELA5C1.f, g

Read the statements below. Then, answer the questions.

   By training, practicing, and concentrating.

1. This is an example of a(n)

   A. run-on   C. independent clause

   B. fragment   D. complete sentence

2. If a correction is needed, choose the best one.
   A. We won. By training, practicing, and concentrating.

   B. By training, practicing, and concentrating, our relay team.

   C. By training, practicing, and concentrating, our relay team won our event.

   D. No correction is needed.

My favorite candy is gumdrops they are delicious.

3. This is an example of a
   A. run-on
   B. fragment
   C. dependent clause
   D. complete sentence

4. If a correction is needed, choose the best one.
   A. My favorite candy is gumdrops, they are delicious.
   B. My favorite candy is gumdrops; they are delicious.
   C. My favorite candy is gumdrops, but they are delicious.
   D. No correction is needed.

PUNCTUATION

In chapter 2, you reviewed using correct **punctuation**. Now, apply what you've practiced to proofreading an essay.

Punctuation may seem like a small detail. However, no punctuation marks—or marks in the wrong places—can change your message. Such errors make your writing hard to read. As you read through your essay, make sure each sentence has an end mark. Check that you have used commas correctly in sentences.

Watch as Sam proofreads his essay to check his punctuation.

As Sam reads through his essay, he sees this sentence.

Then, my teacher showed me how to apply what we did in class to the homework

Sam sees that he needs an end mark after "homework." He fixes his sentence to read:

Then, my teacher showed me how to apply what we did in class to the homework.

Next, he sees this sentence:

I worked hard this year; and I am very proud of myself.

Sam sees that this is a compound sentence. The semicolon and conjunction are not used together; he needs to choose one or the other. He replaces the semicolon with a comma:

I worked hard this year, and I am very proud of myself.

Sam also remembers that his teacher told him to indent the first sentence of each paragraph. He indents and also takes this time to make sure he has used neat handwriting.

Practice 2: Punctuation

ELA5C1.f, g

Proofread the sentences below for punctuation. Choose the answer that is correct.

Basketball is a game anyone can play though some people are better at it than others.

1. A. Basketball is a game, anyone can play though some people are better at it than others.

    B. Basketball is a game anyone can play though, some people are better at it than others.

    C. Basketball is a game anyone can play, though some people are better at it than others.

    D. No correction is needed.

Most children learn to read in kindergarten

2. A. Most children learn to read in kindergarten.

    B. Most children learn to read in kindergarten.

    C. Most children learn to read in kindergarten.

    D. No correction is needed.

I went to the beach with my grandma, and she bought me a pet hermit crab

3. A. I went to the beach with my grandma and she bought me a pet hermit crab.

    B. I went to the beach, with my grandma, and she bought me a pet hermit crab.

    C. I went to the beach with my grandma and, she bought me a pet hermit crab.

    D. No correction is needed.

Jugglers are talented; but they have to practice a lot.

4. A. Jugglers are talented but they have to practice a lot.

    B. Jugglers are talented, but they have to practice a lot.

    C. Jugglers are talented but, they have to practice a lot.

    D. No correction is needed.

VERB USE

As you proofread your essay, check to see that you have **correct verb use**. Each verb should agree with its subject, and the tense of the verb should stay consistent.

CHECKING FOR SUBJECT/VERB AGREEMENT

If the subject is singular, the verb should be singular.

> **Examples:**

Incorrect: Aunt Jennifer and Uncle Simon was the first to arrive.

Correct: <u>Aunt Jennifer and Uncle Simon</u> <u>were</u> the first to arrive.
          (plural subject)   (plural verb)

Incorrect: Everyone in the class were making too much noise.

Correct: <u>Everyone</u> in the class <u>was making</u> too much noise.
      (singular subject)   (singular verb)

CHECKING FOR CONSISTENT TENSE

Check that your verb tense matches the time you are talking about.

> **Examples:**

Incorrect: From the time James learned to walk, he has always tripping a lot.

Correct: From the time James learned to walk, he has always tripped a lot.

Use the past tense of the verb "to trip" since the action began in the past.

Consistent tense also means that verbs in a series will be parallel (alike).

Incorrect: Sonja enjoys running, biking, and to swim.

Correct: Sonja enjoys running, biking, and swimming.

Practice 3:   Verb Use

ELA5C1

Proofread the sentences from Sam's essay for verb use. Choose the best correction, if one is needed.

Since first grade, I have always earn C's in math.

1. A. Since first grade, I have always earned C's in math.

    B. Since first grade, I have always earns C's in math.

    C. Since first grade, I have always have earned C's in math.

    D. No correction is needed.

My A came as a result of a lot of hard work, and I got it by asking questions, getting extra help from my teacher, and practice.

2. A. My A came as a result of a lot of hard work, and I got it by asking questions, getting extra help from my teacher, and to practice.

    B. My A came as a result of a lot of hard work, and I got it by asking questions, getting extra help from my teacher, and practicing.

    C. My A came as a result of a lot of hard work, and I got it by asking questions, get extra help from my teacher, and practice.

    D. No correction is needed.

My teacher gave me extra homework problems so I practice until fractions and word problems was easy!

3. A. My teacher gave me extra homework problems so I was practicing until fractions and word problems was easy!

    B. My teacher gave me extra homework problems so I could practice until fractions and word problems were easy!

    C. My teacher gave me extra homework problems so I practice until fractions and word problems were being easy!

    D. No correction is needed.

Editing the Essay

Then, my teacher explain it all until it made sense.

4. A. Then, my teacher explained it all until it made sense.

   B. Then, my teacher explains it all until it made sense.

   C. Then, my teacher had been explained it all until it made sense.

   D. No correction is needed.

SPELLING AND CAPITALIZATION

As you proofread your essay, check to see that you used correct **spelling** and **capitalization**.

Pay special attention to **homonyms** and other words that are often confused. Homonyms are words that sound alike but are spelled differently and have different meanings.

Commonly Confused Homonyms					
by	our	right	their	to	your
buy	hour	write	there	too	you're
bye			they're	two	

Think about some of the spelling rules you have learned in the past, like "*i* before *e* except after *c*." Apply them as you proofread.

Finally, check your essay for correct use of capital letters. The first word of a sentence should be capitalized. Proper nouns should be capitalized.

> **Examples:**
>
> **Incorrect:** I introduced my Teacher to my Grandmother.
>
> **Correct:** I introduced my teacher to my grandmother.

Practice 4: Spelling and Capitalization

ELA5C1.g

Proofread the sentences from Sam's essay for spelling and capitalization. Choose the best correction.

Since first grade, I have always earn C's in Math.

1. A. Since first Grade, I have always earn C's in Math.

   B. Since first grade, I have Always earn C's in Math.

   C. Since first grade, I have always earn C's in math.

   D. No correction is needed.

GRADE
C+

Copyright © American Book Company. DO NOT DUPLICATE. 1-888-264-5877.

Before, I was quite during math, hoping my teacher would not notice me.

2. A. Before, I was quite during math, hoping my teacher wood not notice me.

   B. Before, I was quite during math, hoping my teacher would no notice me.

   C. Before, I was quiet during math, hoping my teacher would not notice me.

   D. No correction is needed.

Next, I asked my teacher for extra help.

3. A. Next, I asked my Teacher for extra help.

   B. Next, i asked my teacher for extra help.

   C. Next, I asked my teacher for Extra Help.

   D. No correction is needed.

I know what your thinking—who wants more homework?

4. A. I know what you're thinking—who wants more homework?

   B. I know what y'our thinking—who wants more homework?

   C. I know what ye thinking—who wants more homework?

   D. No correction is needed.

The first step I took toward erning an A was to ask questions.

5. A. The first step I took toward erning a A was to ask questions.

   B. The first step I took toward earning an A was to ask questions.

   C. The first step I took toward earning a A was to ask questions.

   D. No correction is needed.

Writing Tip
Do not try to proofred before you are done with bigger changes in your essay. That way, you would miss some errors. Make it a separate last step.

As Sam proofread his essay, he edited to fix errors he found. He also made a few final changes in the words he used to make his writing accurate and interesting. Here is his final essay.

Since first grade, I have always earned C's in math. This year, I was very proud to earn my first A in math. My A came as a result of a lot of hard work, and I got it by asking questions, getting extra help from my teacher, and practicing.

The first step I took toward earning an A was to ask questions. Before, I was quiet during math, hoping my teacher would not notice me. This year, I decided to ask questions about the things I did not understand—fractions and word problems. It worked! When I asked questions in class, my teacher explained until I understood.

Next, I asked my teacher for extra help. I stayed after school twice a week. During that time, my teacher showed me how to apply what we did in class to the homework. I also circled problems from the class work that I did not understand. Then, my teacher explained it all until it made sense.

Finally, I practiced more. My teacher gave me extra homework problems so I could practice until fractions and word problems were easy! I know what you are thinking—who wants more homework? But for me, practice made perfect. I also went back and corrected anything I got wrong from the class work or the homework. All of that practice paid off.

By practicing, getting extra help, and asking questions, I was able to raise my math grade from a C to an A. I worked hard this year, and I am very proud of myself. I learned something besides fractions too. I learned that if I decide to be good at something, I can do it.

CHAPTER 6 SUMMARY

When you look for smaller errors, you are **proofreading**.

In this step of the writing process, you will make sure that all of your **sentences** are complete and have correct **punctuation**.

You will check your **verbs** to be sure that they agree with their subjects and are consistent throughout.

Finally, you will check for correct **spelling** and **capitalization**.

CHAPTER 6 REVIEW

ELA5C1.f, g

Proofread the paragraphs below, looking for errors. Choose the best answers for the questions that follow.

If I could change one thing about my room, I would ask my dad to builds me a loft. A loft would be a perfect retreat! It could be in the corner of my room above my window. I'd like to sleep up there, so I'd need to move my bed. I would also want a ladder to get up there so my little sister could not come mess up my stuff. I would have secret meetings up there with my friends it would be like a clubhouse or an indoor tree house! Maybe we could even rig up a basket on a rope and my mom could send snacks up to us.

My loft would have to be small since my room is not very big. There would be room for my bed and a bookshelf. At least four of my friends could fit up their with me. I wouldn't mind if it was small, it would be my very own place. It would be so cool if I could have a zip line from the loft that went out my window to the tree outside. I don't think my Mom would be so crazy about that, though. She'd probably say it was dangerous. Even without a zip line, a loft would be pretty cool.

If I could change one thing about my room, I would ask my dad to builds me a loft.

1. A. If I could change one thing about my room, I would ask my dad to build me a loft.

   B. If I could change one thing about my room, I will have asked my dad to builds me a loft.

   C. If I could be changing one thing about my room, I would ask my dad to builds me a loft.

   D. No correction is needed.

It could be in the corner of my room above my window.

2. A. It could be in the corner, of my room above my window.

   B. It could be in the Corner of my room above my window.

   C. It could be in the corner of my room; above my window.

   D. No correction is needed.

I would have secret meetings up there with my friends it would be like a clubhouse or an indoor tree house!

3. A. I would have secret meetings up there with my friends. It would be like a clubhouse or an indoor tree house!

   B. I would have secret meetings up there with my friends and it would be like a clubhouse or an indoor tree house!

   C. I would have secret meetings up there with my friends, it would be like a clubhouse or an indoor tree house!

   D. No correction is needed.

Maybe we could even rig up a basket on a rope and my mom could send snacks up to us.

4. A. Maybe we could even rig up a basket; on a rope and my mom could send snacks up to us.

   B. Maybe we could even rig up a basket on a rope, and my mom could send snacks up to us.

   C. Maybe we could even rig up a basket on a rope. And my mom could send snacks up to us.

   D. No correction is needed.

At least four of my friends could fit up their with me.

5. A. At least four of my friends could fit up the with me.

    B. At least four of my friends could fit up they're with me.

    C. At least four of my friends could fit up there with me.

    D. No correction is needed.

I wouldn't mind if it was small, it would be my very own place.

6. A. I wouldn't mind if it was small. It would be my very own place.

    B. I wouldn't mind if it was small it would be my very own place.

    C. I wouldn't mind if it was small; and it would be my very own place.

    D. No correction is needed.

I don't think my Mom would be so crazy about that, though.

7. A. I don't think my mom would be so crazy about that, though.

    B. I don't think My Mom would be so crazy about that, though.

    C. I don't think my Mom would be so Crazy about that, though.

    D. No correction is needed.

She'd probably say, it was dangerous.

8. A. She'd probably say it was dangerous.

    B. She'd probably say it was dangerous.

    C. She'd probably say, and it was dangerous

    D. No correction is needed.

9. You wrote a five-paragraph essay in chapter 4 and revised it in chapter 5. Now it is time to proofread and edit it. Use the proofreading checklist at the beginning of this chapter as a guide. Here is the writing prompt once more:

> Many people continue debating the issue of crime and violence in our society. Explain the steps you would take to reduce crime and violence.

Chapter 7
Narrative Writing

This chapter addresses the Grade 5 Writing Assessment Ideas, Organization, Style, and Conventions rubrics and covers the following GPS standard:

> **ELA5W2 The student demonstrates competence in a variety of genres.**
> The student produces a **narrative** that:
> a. Engages the reader by establishing a context, creating a point of view, and otherwise developing reader interest.
> b. Establishes a plot, point of view, setting, and conflict and/or the significance of events.
> c. Creates an organizing structure.
> d. Includes sensory details and concrete language to develop plot and character.
> e. Excludes extraneous details and inconsistencies.
> h. Provides a sense of closure to the writing.
> i. Lifts the level of language using appropriate strategies including word choice.

In this chapter, you will review and practice some ways to write a good narrative response. You will learn some key ways to help your narrative score well. To see an example of a high-scoring narrative response, as well as one that would get a low score, go to chapter 10, Scoring the Essay.

WHAT IS A NARRATIVE ESSAY?

When you take the Grade 5 Writing Assessment, one type of prompt you could receive is a narrative prompt. It calls for you to write a **narrative essay**. You will know that the prompt is asking for a narrative response if it has certain signal words and phrases. These signals include wording like, "write a story about…" or "write about your experience."

When you write a narrative response, your story might be true. For example, if a prompt asks about something that happened in your life, you can write about what you remember. Look back at Sam's paper in chapters 3 through 6. Sam wrote his response based on recalling when he was most proud of himself. This is called a **personal narrative**.

Sometimes you may not have had an experience in your life that the prompt is asking about. A prompt might also ask about a "what if" situation. In that case, make it up! Write from your imagination. Remember that, when authors write stories, many are made up. You can create an **imaginative story** too.

If you receive a narrative writing prompt, remember these important points.

QUALITIES OF A NARRATIVE

A good narrative essay

- is lively and imaginative.
- has vivid descriptions of people, places, and events.
- includes a setting, characters, a plot with a conflict, and so on—just like any story!
- has a beginning, a middle, and an end.
- can include story elements like foreshadowing, flashback, dialogue, and suspense.
- includes precise language to tell what happens.
- contains logical organization, a variety of correct sentences, and proper grammar and mechanics.

NARRATIVE WRITING CHECKLIST

You may receive a narrative prompt when you take the Grade 5 Writing Assessment. If you do, along with it, you will get this narrative writing checklist. It is a good reminder of what you need to do as you write.

Student Writing Checklist for Narrative Writing

☐ **Prepare Yourself to Write**
Read the writing topic carefully.
Brainstorm for ideas using your imagination and/or personal experiences.
Decide what ideas to include and how to organize them.
Write only in English.

☐ **Make Your Paper Meaningful**
Use your imagination and/or personal experiences to provide specific details.
Tell a complete story.
Create a plot or order of events.
Describe the setting and characters in your story.
Write a story that has a beginning, middle, and end.

☐ **Make Your Paper Interesting to Read**
Think about what would be interesting to the reader.
Use a lively writing voice that holds the interest of your reader.
Use descriptive words.
Use different types of sentences.

☐ **Make Your Paper Easy to Read**
Write in paragraph form.
Use transition words.
Write in complete and correct sentences.
Capitalize, spell, and punctuate correctly.
Make sure your subjects and verbs agree.

GRABBING THE READER

Think about some of the stories that you have read. Which ones were the most interesting? What made you want to keep reading? Sometimes, a statement or question at the start makes a reader want to find out more. Other times, the characters are interesting, and a reader wants to see what they will do and say. Whatever you decide to use, you want to **grab the reader**. Look at these examples of how a story might begin.

> **Example 1:** Once, there was a little girl who was sad because she was poor, so she dreamed about a better life.

> **Example 2:** Dreams are all some people have…one sad, poor girl knew this, so she dreamed so hard that someone listened.

The first example is pretty boring. It simply tells that the story will be about a poor girl who dreams of a better life. The second example, though, first offers an observation ("Dreams are all some people have…"). This makes the reader think about how poor some people are. It then reveals the story is about one person ("one sad, poor girl") and that something remarkable might happen because of her dreams. The words "someone listened" stir up curiosity. Now, the reader wants to find out what will happen!

Other ways that you can grab the reader include the following.

Ways to Grab the Reader	
Method	**Example**
Ask a question that makes the reader want to know what you're talking about.	Have you ever done something just because someone told you not to?
Begin with an uncommon trait of your main character.	Alex had always been curious about clocks, so he took all of them apart.
Start with an action that makes the reader wonder why it happened.	When the invitation arrived in the mail, I threw it in the trash right away.

DEVELOPING THE STORY

When you write a narrative, you should consider the **elements** of a story. Let's talk about some of these.

PLOT

Naturally, a story needs an interesting **plot**. What happens in a narrative is like the banana in a banana split—without it, the ice cream, chocolate sauce, nuts, and cherry on top may still be delicious, but it's not a banana split anymore. The same is true for a narrative. The characters, setting, and descriptions might be lovely. However, without a good plot, it's just not a story.

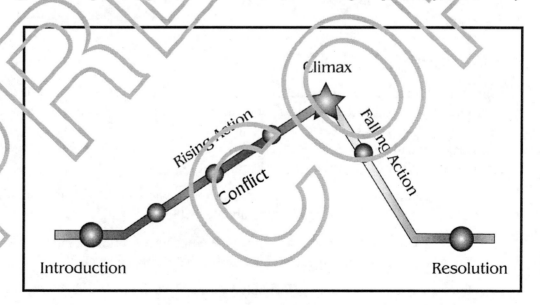

When you write your narrative, think about stories that you have read. Most have a similar plot sequence. There is an **introduction**, in which we learn a little about characters and the setting. Then, the action builds, and we may learn about a **conflict** (a problem to be solved). The action builds to a **climax** (a turning point in the story). After that, we see a **resolution** (the ending of the story), when everything is solved or returns to normal.

For an example, look at Sam's final narrative essay in chapter 6. His first paragraph is the introduction, in which we find out about his struggles with math. We find out what he did to improve throughout the story. The conflict is the fact that he wanted an A but was getting C's. The climax of the story is implied (hinted at)—when he takes tests and does homework after all of his preparation. The resolution is that he reaches his goal and gets the A!

SETTING

The plot needs a place and time to happen. This is the **setting** of the story. For example, a personal narrative takes place sometime in your life. It happens in some place where you have been. An imaginative story can take place anytime, including the future. It can happen anywhere, including a made-up place. When you write, you need to provide clues about when and where the story is happening. You should use precise and vivid words to describe the setting in detail. Look at how much more descriptive Example 2 is than Example 1.

> **Example 1:** I was sitting in my very messy bedroom.

> **Example 2:** I sat on the only clean patch of the floor in my bedroom. Around me were dirty clothes, papers from school, half-eaten candy bars, and games with missing pieces.

POINT OF VIEW

Another aspect to think about is what point of view your story will take. For the most part, a personal narrative is told in **first person** since it is a story that you tell about something that happened to you. You will use first-person pronouns, saying, "*I* did *this*" and "this happened to *me*."

If you are writing an imaginative story, you can still write in first person. However, the character telling the story does not necessarily have to be you. For example, Mark Twain wrote *The Adventures of Huckleberry Finn* in first person, from the point of view of Huck. That doesn't mean Mark Twain is Huck!

Mark Twain

Or, you can choose to use **third person**. In third-person point of view, you can talk about all the characters using third-person pronouns like *he*, *she*, and *they*.

CHARACTERS

Don't forget that your story needs **characters**. If you are in the story, then you are one of the characters. Be sure to tell the reader important things about other characters. This includes why they are in the story. It also might include what they look like or how they act.

LITERARY DEVICES

A narrative can be more fun to read if it contains some **literary devices**. These include flashback, foreshadowing, dialogue, and suspense. Look at these examples of using these devices in a narrative.

Literary Devices in a Narrative		
Device	**Definition**	**Example**
flashback	A **flashback** tells a past event. It is usually something a character remembers.	The bully walked toward me. That's when I remembered the whistle in my pocket. In gym class, I had stuck it in my jeans, meaning to give it to Coach Harrison on the way out of the locker room. It would come in handy now!
foreshadowing	**Foreshadowing** gives a clue about something that will happen later in the story.	All day, Randi had the feeling that something unusual was about to happen.
dialogue	When characters talk, we see what they say set off in quotation marks. This is called **dialogue**.	The teacher looked at my report. "This is the best work you've ever done," he said.
suspense	**Suspense** is uncertainty about how things will turn out.	The sky was getting dark. Would my new shoes be ruined? What would Mom say? I started to run toward home.

Practice 1: Developing the Story

I LA5W2.a, b NAR

1. In a narrative essay, the first paragraph should

    A. grab the reader.

    B. introduce the characters.

    C. tell what the story will be about.

    D. all of the above

2. When you describe something that happened before a story began, you are using
   A. dialogue.
   B. flashback.
   C. suspense.
   D. foreshadowing.

3. What is one way to make the setting of a story interesting?
   A. Repeat information about the setting in each paragraph.
   B. Be sure to describe setting details in an organized way.
   C. Use vivid descriptions of when and where the story takes place.
   D. Ask many questions about the setting to create some suspense.

4. Read the following prompts. Each prompt calls for a narrative response. Choose a prompt, and write a narrative essay.
   - Use the lists in this chapter (like "Qualities of a Narrative Essay" and "Ways to Grab the Reader") to find ways to improve your narrative.
   - Review chapters 3, 4, 5, and 6 to work through the writing process to a final version of the essay.
   - Keep your essay in your writing folder or journal. You will practice scoring it in chapter 10.

Narrative Writing Prompts

1. What is the first thing you remember from when you were small? Write a story about what you remember. Talk about why you think the memory has lasted and what made the event so memorable.

2. People sometimes disagree, and everyone thinks he or she is right. Did you ever disagree with someone but find out that person was right? Think about what the argument was and which side you took. How did you feel when you realized the other side was right? Write about your experience.

3. Imagine that you are granted the ability to talk to animals for one day. What animals would you talk with, and what would you talk about? Write a story about your day.

4. Think about a time in your life when something bad happened, but it turned out to be a good thing. Include details about the negative event and how it turned into something positive. Write about your experience.

For more practice, choose more prompts, and write essays in response to them. Keep these in your writing folder or journal.

ORGANIZING

In previous chapters, you learned about ways to organize ideas and present them in a logical order. In chapter 3, you saw how to get your ideas on paper and to choose a focus and purpose.

In chapter 4, you learned about the importance of **five-paragraph essay** structure. Like any other essay, a narrative needs the following:

- an introduction (paragraph one)
- supporting ideas (paragraphs two through four)
- a conclusion (paragraph five)

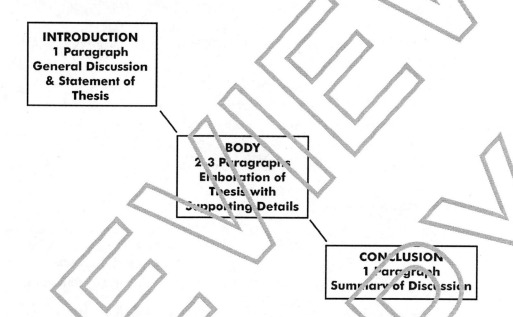

Also in chapter 4, you read about **organizational patterns**. You saw that chronological order is the usual way to write a narrative. Did you know that you can use other patterns as well? Any of the patterns in chapter 4 can be used to write a narrative. It all depends on the topic of your story. Here is an example of using a different pattern for a specific prompt.

Say that Cyndi needs to write a narrative in response to the following prompt.

> Everyone has some good days and some bad days. Think of when you had a really great day. What happened, and how did you feel? Write about your experience.

What would be the best way for Cyndi to organize her narrative?

A. chronological

B. cause and effect

C. similarity and difference

D. question and answer

In this case, a good way to organize might be cause and effect. The whole story has to do with why Cyndi had such a great day. So, she can discuss reasons (causes) for the day being so good. She can also discuss the effect of how she felt.

After you read a narrative prompt, think about what you will write in each paragraph. Remember the five-paragraph essay structure. Also, think about the best organization pattern for the topic. It may not always be chronological order!

Practice 2: Organizing

ELA5W2.c NAR

Read the following narrative prompts. For each one, decide what would be the best pattern to choose when writing a response. Then, briefly write your reasons for choosing that pattern.

Ramon received the following narrative prompt.

> Every member of a family fills a special place. Some children were born first and some in the middle. Some have many siblings. Others may be the only child in their family. Write a paper about your place in your family. Tell what advantages or disadvantages it gives you.

1. What would be the best way for Ramon to organize his narrative?

   A. chronological

   B. cause and effect

   C. similarity and difference

   D. question and answer

2. Briefly explain why you made this choice.

Alissa has to write an essay based on the following narrative prompt.

> Imagine that you and a friend are working on a science project, and you accidentally build a time machine! You can go to three places before the machine stops working. Write a story about what places and times you visit and what happens in each one.

3. Which pattern should Alissa use to organize her essay?

   A. chronological

   B. cause and effect

   C. similarity and difference

   D. question and answer

4. Explain why you chose this pattern.

Miranda needs to write an essay based on the following prompt.

> It is an honor to be recognized for something you do well. Write a story about a time when you were honored with an award or other recognition. What did you do to earn this honor? What were you given as an award, and who gave it to you? Include details about events that led to this honor as well as what happened afterward.

5. What would be the best way for Miranda to organize her narrative?

6. Explain why you chose this pattern.

WRITING A CONCLUSION

When you get to the end of your essay, you want to make sure you have a strong **conclusion**. Because you are writing a narrative, you might think that the story can just end. Well, there's a little more to it than that!

The conclusion of a narrative needs to tie up loose ends and provide a clear ending. A conclusion should always do the following:

- briefly summarize the narrative
- refer back to the main point in the introduction

A conclusion can also do other things. Here are some other ways you can make your conclusion a strong one.

What a Conclusion Can Do	
Description	**Example**
Tell why the experience or event is important.	I'm glad I learned to swim that day. Now, I don't need to be afraid to go near the water.
Say "goodbye" to the reader with an appropriate closing.	The excitement is over, and life is back to normal. Now, we can all just smile when we remember what happened.
Give the reader something to think about or something to do.	So, next time you want to do an extreme stunt, consider what happened to me!

Practice 3: Conclusions

ELA5W2.h NAR

Read these concluding paragraphs. For each one, tell what the conclusion does.

That's how I learned not to judge people by what they have or how they dress. At the time, I didn't know how important a lesson this was. Since then, I have made many friends, and I don't think the "old me" would have been friends with them. I don't know what I would do without them now. I'm glad I'm not the old me now.

1. This conclusion
    A. tells why the experience or event is important.
    B. says "goodbye" to the reader with an appropriate closing.
    C. gives the reader something to think about or something to do.
    D. none of the above

Most people don't have everything they want. However, in that soup kitchen, I saw that many people don't have what they need—the most important things like food, shelter, and a family. Next time you're having a bad day, remember that there are people who have no friends, no home, and no food. Then, do something to help!

2. This conclusion
    A. tells why the experience or event is important.
    B. says "goodbye" to the reader with an appropriate closing.
    C. gives the reader something to think about or something to do.
    D. none of the above

That was a wonderful birthday party. It was great that my cousins and friends chipped in to get me such a great gift. Whenever I use it, I always think of that day.

3. This conclusion
    A. tells why the experience or event is important.
    B. says "goodbye" to the reader with an appropriate closing.
    C. gives the reader something to think about or something to do.
    D. none of the above

Let's say that your essay is well organized. You have developed the story well. It has a good plot, clear setting, and interesting characters. You have added a strong conclusion. Are you done? Is there anything else you can do?

Yes, you can do more to improve your essay. Here are a few ways to improve a narrative.

USING THE RIGHT WORDS

A great way to make your narrative jump off the page is to use vivid **descriptive details**. Think about painting a picture for the reader. Can you see, hear, smell, taste, and feel what's going on in the story?

To do this, use words that appeal to the senses. The following are just a few examples. You can find many more using a thesaurus.

Descriptive Words That Appeal to the Senses
Sight words
brilliant, dim, frayed, gargantuan, glossy, inflated, layered, miniature, oblong, oval, silvery, spacious 
Sound words
clang, chime, deafening, echo, howl, raucous, repetitious, screech, snarl, squeal, twang, wail
Touch words
bumpy, delicate, fractured, freezing, grooved, leathery, mushy, rough, scalding, slimy, slippery, smooth
Taste words
acidic, bitter, chalky, flaky, juicy, metallic, peppery, refreshing, sour, spicy, syrupy, tangy
Smell words
acrid, aromatic, burnt, flowery, fragrant, fresh, lemony, minty, moldy, musty, pungent, stale

Look at this example from a student essay. This excerpt describes a setting.

> Sometimes I go to a gym down the street with my big sister. She works out there. I usually ride a stationary bike until she's done. It's fun sometimes to watch big guys lifting big weights. They make funny faces! I don't like having to go in the locker room to use the restroom because all the sweaty clothes make it stinky. But I do like the main room. It's full of TVs and music playing.

It's not a bad description, but more descriptive language would really help. When telling about a setting, you want a reader to picture the scene. The same is true for describing a character—the reader should be able to see what the person is like. Take a look at the revised description. It tells us more about the gym and uses words that appear to the senses. Notice that the writer combined sentences in different ways to fit the new information.

Sometimes I walk four blocks with my big sister to a gym where she works out. I usually take a leisurely ride on a stationary bike until she's done huffing and puffing around the room on other exercise machines. It's hilarious sometimes to watch burly guys lifting huge weights. They scrunch up their faces as they build their biceps! I loathe having to go in the dank locker room to use the restroom because all the sweaty clothes create a putrid odor. But I do like the bright and lively main room. It's full of TVs and energetic music playing.

In addition to vivid description, you want to use the right words. The choices you make should be precise. **Precise word choice** means that you use just the right word to say what you mean. Look at these examples.

Example 1: I got down off the desk when the mouse ran away.

What would be a more precise way to write what happened? Look at Example 2.

Example 2: I hopped down off the desk when the mouse scampered across the floor and out the door.

Notice how precise wording and vivid description go hand in hand. Usually, when you choose the right words, you will also paint a better picture for the reader. So, think about the words you use in every sentence.

Practice 4: Using the Right Words

ELA5W2.d, NAR

Take out the essay that you wrote earlier in response to Practice 1 in this chapter. Read it over, and look for ways to improve descriptions and include more precise words. Remember, use words that appeal to the senses. Choose precise words to say what you mean.

DELETING WHAT IS NOT NEEDED

As you work at the right words to include, also look for those that you don't need. Read your essay again. See if there is anything that doesn't belong, and **delete unneeded details**. Is there too much description about a certain place or person? Are there phrases or sentences that repeat things? If a word, phrase, or sentence is not needed in the story, take it out!

Read this example paragraph from a narrative essay.

> We took the subway to the city. Once we were in the city, the guide reminded us to stay together. We walked for about two hours and several miles around the city. We walked a long way. The first place we stopped was a coffee shop that Martin Luther King Jr. has visited. We also saw the city hall and an old church. The church had been there for over 150 years.

What do you notice in this paragraph? Think about what you would change.

- The writer uses "to the city" and "in the city" in the first two sentences. When you see the same words close to one another, decide if they are needed in both places.

- Later, the writers talks about walking around the city. Two sentences mention this. Are both needed? Which one is more descriptive?

- Toward the end of the paragraph, the writer describes the church in two ways—it was "old" and it "had been there for over 150 years." Are both needed? Which description is more precise?

Here is a revised version of this paragraph.

> We took the subway to the city. Once we were there, the guide reminded us to stay together. We walked for about two hours and several miles around the city. The first place we stopped was a coffee shop that Martin Luther King Jr. has visited. We also saw the city hall and a church that had been there for over 150 years.

Practice 5: Deleting What Is Not Needed

ELA5W2.e NAR

Once again, take out the essay that you wrote in response to Practice 1. Read it over. Look for any repeated words, phrases, and sentences. Can you delete some? Can you combine some sentences that have similar information? Remember to keep the more descriptive and precise wording.

Use the steps you learned about in this chapter when you write a narrative response. Go to chapter 10 to see an example of a narrative that would score high on the Grade 5 Writing Assessment. There is also an example of a narrative that would not score well. What changes would you make in the low-scoring essay?

CHAPTER 7 SUMMARY

A **narrative essay** is a story. When a prompt asks for a narrative response, you can write from memory, or you can use your imagination.

To **grab the reader**, be sure to begin with something interesting. Three ways to do that include asking a **question**, beginning with an uncommon **character trait**, or starting with an **action** that makes the reader wonder why it happened.

Develop the story by including elements like a good **plot**, a well-described **setting**, the right **point of view, characters**, and some **literary devices**.

Organize the story logically. Use the **organizational pattern** that best fits the topic of your story. Usually you will use **chronological** order, but you may also use **cause and effect, similarity and difference**, or **question and answer**.

Remember to end with a **strong conclusion**. Your conclusion should summarize your ideas and related back to the main point.

Using **description details and precise words** will help your essay be clear and interesting.

Finally, **delete what is not needed**. This keeps your narrative focused and coherent.

CHAPTER 7 REVIEW

ELA5W2.a, b, c, d, e, h, I NAR

A. Read questions 1 through 6, and choose the best answer for each.

Say that Davey needs to write a narrative in response to the following prompt.

> You have been made the head of a toy company for one day. Write a story about what happens during your day in this position.

1. What would be the best way for Davey to organize his narrative?

    A. chronological

    B. cause and effect

    C. similarity and difference

    D. question and answer

2. A narrative can use some literary devices, like foreshadowing, flashback, and

    A. chronology.

    B. suspense.

    C. humor.

    D. none of the above

3. Narrative essays should use the elements of a story. These include plot, point of view, and

    A. ending.

    B. order.

    C. setting.

    D. timing.

Read this sentence.

The pie smelled good and
looked tasty.

4. What is the best way to make this sentence more descriptive and interesting?
    A. The pie on the window sill smelled good and looked tasty.
    B. A pie that I saw smelled so good and looked very tasty.
    C. The apple pie smelled delicious and looked mouth-watering.
    D. Some pie was smelling nice and looking pretty good too.

Read this sentence.

Sara has brown hair and whistles a lot.

5. What is the best way to make the wording more precise?
    A. Sara has lustrous brown hair and whistles musical little tunes all day long.
    B. My best friend Sara has long, straight, brown hair and whistles as she walks.
    C. That girl Sara has nice brown hair, and she is always whistling a lot.
    D. My friend Sara has brown hair that's long and likes to whistles all the time.

6. What should every conclusion do?
    A. have a brief summary of the story
    B. refer to the main point in the introduction
    C. say "goodbye" to the reader
    D. all of the above

B. Read the following writing prompt. Then, use your own paper to do the activities that follow.

> Do many people visit your town or city? Write a story about what a tourist can do in your town or city. Tell what a typical day seeing the sights would include.

7. What would you write about your town or city? Do some prewriting, and create an outline of what you would write in your narrative response. This question is about the best organizational pattern to use.

Introduction _____

First paragraph _____

Second paragraph _____

Third paragraph _____

Conclusion _____

8. What story elements would you use? Fill in the blanks with notes about what you can include. How would you use each of these elements?

Plot _____

Conflict _____

Setting _____

Point of view _____

Characters _____

Literary devices _____

9. Now, review your notes from the questions above. Write a five-paragraph essay about a typical day in your city. Use the Student Writing Checklist for Narrative Writing to help you stay on track.

Chapter 8
Informational Writing

This chapter addresses the Grade 5 Writing Assessment Ideas, Organization, Style, and Conventions rubrics and covers the following GPS standard:

ELA5W2 The student demonstrates competence in a variety of genres.

The student produces **informational** writing (e.g., report, procedures, correspondence) that:

a. Engages the reader by establishing a context, creating a speaker's voice, and otherwise developing reader interest.

b. Develops a controlling idea that conveys a perspective on a subject.

c. Creates an organizing structure appropriate to a specific purpose, audience, and context.

d. Includes appropriate facts and details.

e. Excludes extraneous details and inappropriate information.

f. Uses a range of appropriate strategies, such as providing facts and details, describing or analyzing the subject, and narrating a relevant anecdote.

h. Provides a sense of closure to the writing.

i. Lifts the level of language using appropriate strategies including word choice.

In this chapter you will practice informational writing. To see an example of a high-scoring informational essay, as well as one that would get a low score, go to chapter 10, Scoring the Essay.

WHAT IS INFORMATIONAL WRITING?

An **informational essay** (also called an expository essay) is one that informs. Like your textbooks, it explains something. Think about how your science book explains an atom. Think about how your history book explains America's early stages. An informational essay also can tell how to do a process or how something works.

Informational writing can

- share information
- tell how to do something
- explain how something works

You can find different kinds of informational writing both in school and in everyday life.

Examples of informational writing:

- a manual that shows how to assemble and use a skateboard
- a school newspaper article about a recent scout outing
- a research paper about new ways to treat cancer
- an essay comparing different kinds of dinosaurs

An effective informational essay has several parts. These parts work together to inform the reader about the topic.

A good informational essay

- has a clear main idea.
- is structured and organized in a way that keeps the main idea clear.
- uses effective details to develop and support the idea.
- keeps the reader's interest.
- uses descriptive and precise words and has correct grammar and spelling.

INFORMATIONAL WRITING CHECKLIST

If the prompt you receive for the Grade 5 Writing Assessment is an informational writing prompt, you will also get this checklist. Use it to help you create your essay. It contains guidelines for what to keep in mind as you write.

Student Writing Checklist for Informational Writing

☐ **Prepare Yourself to Write**
Read the writing topic carefully.
Brainstorm for ideas.
Decide what ideas to include and how to organize them.
Write only in English.

☐ **Make Your Paper Meaningful**
Use your knowledge and/or personal experiences that are related to the topic.
Explain your ideas.
Develop your main idea with supporting details.
Organize your ideas in a clear order.
Write an informational paper and stay on topic.

☐ **Make Your Paper Interesting to Read**
Think about what would be interesting to the reader.
Use a lively writing voice to hold the interest of your reader.
Use descriptive words.
Use different types of sentences.

☐ **Make Your Paper Easy to Read**
Write in paragraph form.
Use transition words.
Write in complete and correct sentences.
Capitalize, spell, and punctuate correctly.
Make sure your subjects and verbs agree.

MAKING IT INTERESTING

You've probably heard the saying, "Don't judge a book by its cover." It means that if a book's cover looks good (or not) it does not necessarily mean that a book will be good (or not). However, a book's cover is the first impression. It is the first thing that inspires **reader interest**.

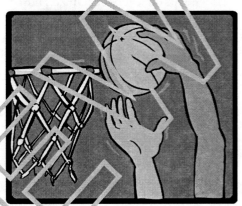

First impressions are important. Give the reader of your essay a good first impression by starting your essay in an interesting way. You can do this by starting your essay in a way that makes the reader want to read more. Read the two examples below. Each example is the beginning of an informational essay.

Example 1: Some people are good at sports. This essay will show you what you need to know to succeed at basketball.

Example 2: With five seconds left on the clock, Jameson drove the length of the court and drained a three-point shot. The amazed audience wondered, "How did he do that?"

Example 1 tells what the essay will be about, but it does so in an uninteresting way. People who are not interested in basketball might not care to read on.

Example 2 pulls the reader in with a story. Using a person's name and describing an action creates an exciting beginning. Using a brief story can build a reader's interest in a topic. It makes the reader want to read on.

Now you need to keep the reader's interest for the rest of the essay. You can do this by using vivid scenes like Example 2. Bringing people, action, and description into an essay helps keep a reader's interest.

Practice 1: Making It Interesting

ELA5W2.a INF

Choose three topics from the list that follows. For each, make up a short (two to three sentences) story that you could include in an informational essay. Be sure to consider what would be interesting to a reader. Write your brief story on your own paper or in your writing journal.

Informational Topics	
amusement parks	football
babysitting	sewing
baking	swimming
chores	video games

MAIN IDEA AND SUPPORTING DETAILS

A good essay makes a point. The **main idea** of an essay is the main point the author wants to make. In informational writing, the point might be to teach how to do CPR. Or, it might be to explain how exercise burns calories. Whatever the point, it is important to **stick to the point** and **support the point** with relevant examples.

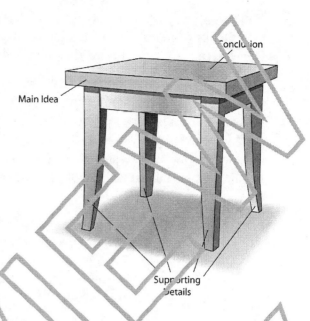

Informational writing includes facts and details to support the point. When you do informational writing for class, it usually includes some research. You can use books, Internet sites, interviews, and other sources to add facts and examples that support your point. When you are writing for the Grade 5 Writing Assessment, you will not have access to these sources. However, there are still ways to support what you say. You can support your point by including what you know, such as the following:

- facts
- statistics
- descriptive details
- definitions
- analysis
- evaluation
- personal anecdotes

Choose examples that support your point. Make it clear to the reader what the connection is between your main idea and the supporting details. Ask yourself if your ideas and your support will make sense to the reader. Read the two examples that follow.

Example 1: Fish make good first pets. They are colorful. They don't cost much to keep, but the tank and filter and gravel are expensive when you first buy them. My first fish died the day after I brought it home. Fish are friendly to have around.

Example 2: Fish make good first pets. They are inexpensive and require little care. Even a young child can sprinkle fish food into the tank twice a day. Feeding the fish, changing the water, and cleaning the bowl can teach a person the responsibilities of owning a pet. If you are looking for your first pet, start with a fish!

The main idea of both paragraphs is the same: fish make good first pets. However, the details in Example 2 support this idea better than the details in Example 1. Let's look at each example.

In Example 1, each sentence does relate to fish, but none of these details support the point. The detail that "they are colorful" may be true, but it does not show how fish make good pets. Telling how expensive the supplies are is a negative idea. It does not help support the point. Sharing that the writer's fish died after one day will not convince anyone that a fish makes a good pet. The statement that, "fish are friendly to have around" may be true, but it is a general comment. Supporting details are more specific.

Example 2 uses details well to support the point. Ideas like "inexpensive" and "require little care" are attractive for a new pet owner. The brief list of duties (feeding, changing the water, cleaning the bowl) sounds easy. The writer shows how taking care of a fish is a simple way to learn how to care for a pet.

Example 2 uses effective details. All of the details support the main idea of the paragraph. Details that support the main idea help build a strong essay.

Remember:

- Each sentence of a paragraph should support the main idea of that paragraph.
- Each paragraph of the essay should, in turn, support the main point of the essay.

Practice 2: Main Idea and Supporting Details

ELA5W2.b, f INF

Read the paragraphs below. Then, answer the questions.

An oil spill has several effects upon water animals. Oil kills the fish other animals eat, making food hard to find. Oil sticks to the animals' coats and feathers, making it hard for them to swim or fly. Oil spills can mean suffering and death for water animals.

What is the main idea?

A. how bad oil tastes to animals

B. what happens when an animal eats oil

C. how to clean oil off an animal

D. the effects of oil spills on water animals

2. Which would be a good example to include in this paragraph to support the main idea?

    A. Oil can poison animals that accidentally eat it.

    B. Oil companies who spill should be fined.

    C. Oil is a valuable natural resource.

    D. Oil is expensive because it is hard to find.

> When making cutout cookies, rolling out the dough is an important step. Cold dough is easier to roll, so keep the dough in the refrigerator. Sprinkle flour on the surface where you will roll out the dough. Put the dough on the surface, then begin pushing and rolling it with a floured rolling pin. When the dough is about 1/3" thick, it is time to use the cookie cutters.

3. What is the main idea?

    A. the best shapes for cutout cookies

    B. how to roll out cookie dough

    C. why cold dough is best

    D. how to mix cookie dough

4. Which would be a good detail to include in this paragraph to support the main idea?

    A. Cookies taste best with milk.

    B. Some people are allergic to cookies.

    C. If the dough sticks to the rolling pin, sprinkle on a little flour.

    D. Cookies take a long time to bake, but the wait it certainly worth it.

5. Choose one of the brief stories you wrote for Practice 1. Write an informational essay that teaches or informs the reader about the topic. Remember to stick to your main idea. Support your main point with details, including the brief story from Practice 1.

ORGANIZING

In chapter 4, you learned about **five paragraph essay** structure. Like all essays, informational essays can follow this structure. Your informational essay will begin with an introduction in paragraph one. Paragraphs two through four will be the body of the essay. Paragraph five will be the conclusion.

As you read in chapter 4, there are several ways of **organizing** an essay. Some ways are chronological, cause and effect, compare and contrast, and question and answer. Informational essays can use any of these patterns of organization.

In an informational essay, a writer could use organizational patterns in the following ways:

Organization	Purpose	Example
chronological	describe a process step by step	how to bake oatmeal cookies
cause and effect	analyze the consequences of an action	how pollution affects birds
compare and contrast	show how things are alike and different	saltwater and freshwater fish
question and answer	explain a topic by posing and answering questions	why it is important to study for tests

How you choose to organize your informational essay depends on your topic. For example, if you are describing a process, chronological order is often the best choice. Other topics might use other patterns.

Read the essay prompt below.

> Think back to when you were in first grade. What did you do in school each day? Now, think about being a fifth grader. How is school the same? How is it different? Write an essay discussing the similarities and differences of life in first grade and life in fifth grade.

What would be the best way to organize this essay? If you said compare and contrast, you're right! The prompt asks you to discuss things that are the same and different in first and fifth grades. Organizing this essay using compare and contrast allows you to answer the question by focusing on the similarities and differences between the two grades.

Practice 3: Organizing
ELA5W2.c INF

1. In Practice 2, you wrote an informational essay. Which organizational pattern did you use? Which other patterns could you have used? Explain why you chose the pattern you did.

2. In looking at your essay, you might see that a different pattern might be better. For example, maybe you wrote about how to do chores using a chronological pattern. Maybe it would be more interesting to use cause and effect to show what advantages (or disadvantages) there are for doing chores. Rewrite your essay using the new organization pattern.

WRITING A CONCLUSION

The **conclusion** is the last section of the essay. It is your final chance to leave an impression on the reader. A good conclusion sums of the main point of the essay in a compelling way. It leaves the reader thinking about the ideas you presented. It also restates what the reader learned by reading your essay.

Read the two essay conclusions below. Both conclude an essay about solving overcrowding on earth by creating a place for people to live on the moon.

Example 1

People could end up living on the moon one day. Now that I think about it, I'd like that because I could get away from my brother. We need to build space stations for lots of people. Plus, it would cost a lot to ship food through space! Anyway, that will probably not happen for a long time.

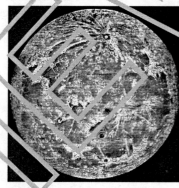

Example 2

Living on the moon may one day be a reality. Before that can happen, scientists will need to develop the technology and overcome the high costs. While moon life could be a solution to the problems we face living on a crowded earth, it would be a very different way of life. If you had a chance to live in a new community on the moon, would you go?

Example 1 is not an effective conclusion. It contains details that belong in the body of the essay. It does not tell why living on the moon is an option. It is not clear what the main points of the essay were. The last sentence says that the ideas in the essay are not worth thinking about since moon life is so far in the future.

Example 2 is an effective conclusion. It restates the main ideas from the essay. This conclusion sums up the main point of the essay and then ends by asking a question that makes the reader think.

Practice 4:   Writing a Conclusion

ELA5W2.h INF

Read the conclusions that follow. Then, choose the best final sentence. For each question, write an explanation of why you made the choice you did.

1. Crossing guards provide a great service to our school. They manage the traffic at every intersection near our school, keeping speeds down. They make the streets safer for all children who walk to school.

    A. Next time you pass a crossing guard, say thank you!

    B. Not all schools have crossing guards, though.

    C. I don't really like the crossing guard who works on my street.

    D. Having crossing guards cost too much money.

2. Both spring and fall are fun seasons. The fall is cooler and the leaves turn vibrant colors. The holidays include Halloween and Thanksgiving, and football is on TV. On the other hand, spring is a time when everything blooms, and we can look forward to summer.

    A. It's hard to decide which season is my favorite.

    B. All four seasons have something that people like and dislike.

    C. Though these two seasons are different, both are enjoyable.

    D. Summer is the best season, though, because there is no school.

3. Being too young to vote does not have to keep a kid out of politics. There are many ways for kids to get involved, including watching political speeches, making campaign signs, and discussing elections with parents.

    A. It's too bad kids can't run for president.

    B. How are you involved with politics?

    C. If you don't have a TV, read the speeches in the newspaper.

    D. Kids should be allowed to vote.

USING THE RIGHT WORDS

How can you make your informational essay stand out? One way is to **choose the right words**. There are certain types of words that can help you keep a reader's interest while making your writing more clear.

Descriptive words make your writing both interesting and accurate. Say that you are writing instructions for baking cupcakes. You will need adjectives to describe what the cupcakes should look like when they are done. Descriptive words help the reader to follow your instructions correctly.

Descriptive words make any type of writing come alive. Adjectives and adverbs add life to writing. A reader who can see, smell, hear, taste, and touch what you are talking about will take more interest in your essay. Refer back to page 100 in chapter 7 to see sample words that appeal to the senses.

Read the examples below.

Example 1:

Daffodils are flowers that grow from bulbs. There are many varieties of daffodils, and they come in many different colors. Daffodils have petals and trumpets. A bunch of daffodils makes a nice bouquet.

Example 2:

A daffodil is a spring flower that grows from a bulb. There are many varieties of daffodils. The most common colors are yellow, white, and orange. Some daffodils are one color and have simple petals and a simple trumpet. Others have a combination of colors, layers of petals, and a ruffled trumpet. A bunch of daffodils makes a lovely spring bouquet.

Notice how Example 1 uses little descriptive language. Example 2 uses language that is descriptive and specific. Thanks to this descriptive language, the reader gets a clearer idea of the topic.

Just as important as using descriptive words is using correct words. **Precise words** make your meaning and ideas clear. They help your reader to understand your point. Look at these examples.

Example 1: Stir the pudding until it's done.

Example 2: Using a whisk, stir the pudding until large bubbles begin to come to the surface, then turn off the heat.

In Example 1, the writer does not tell what makes the pudding "done." Example 2 uses precise words. It tells exactly what to look for. You will notice that precise words are also descriptive words. These two kinds of words work together to help a reader understand the topic.

Practice 5:   Using the Right Words

ELA5W2.i INF

Look back at the informational essay you wrote. Revise it to include words that are descriptive and precise. Remember to choose words that are interesting and also help your reader understand your point.

WHAT TO INCLUDE, WHAT TO TAKE OUT

While descriptive words help a writer paint a picture, there is such a thing as too much of a good thing! Some things in an essay need to be described in detail, and some do not. Read through your essay to **take out unneeded details**. As you think about what belongs in your essay, consider what a reader needs to know to understand your point.

Read the paragraph below.

Hurricane Katrina was a devastating storm. I remember that I was standing in the kitchen when my mom told me about it. Many people lost their homes and everything in them. The storm did billions of dollars worth of damage. Not so many people in Georgia were affected by the storm. It has been a few years since Katrina, but people in New Orleans are still cleaning up and rebuilding.

This paragraph contains some details that are not needed. It does not help a reader's understanding to know where the writer was when he heard the news. It does not help the writer's point to include, "Not so many people in Georgia were affected by the storm." Deleting these details helps keep the focus on the main point of the paragraph.

Now, read the paragraph with these unneeded details taken out.

Hurricane Katrina was a devastating storm. Many people lost their homes and everything in them. The storm did billions of dollars worth of damage. It has been a few years since Katrina, but people in New Orleans are still cleaning up and rebuilding.

Now, the focus of the paragraph stays clear. Only facts and details relating to the point are included.

Practice 6: What to Include, What to Take Out

ELA5W2.d, e INF

Look back at the informational essay you wrote. Review it for any extra information. Delete unneeded details. If a detail does not support your main idea or help the reader understand your point, take it out.

Chapter 8 Summary

An **informational essay** explains, describes, or teaches.

To **make it interesting**, begin in a way that gets the reader's interest. Using people, events, and action are some ways to make it interesting.

Stay focused on your **main idea**. Stick to the point, and support your point with effective details.

Organize your essay in a way that makes sense for the topic.

Use the **conclusion** to restate what your reader has learned. Keep the reader thinking about your main idea.

Use words that are **descriptive** and **precise** to help the reader understand your point.

Delete unneeded details that do not help make to your point.

CHAPTER 8 REVIEW

ELA5W2 a, b, c, d, e, f, h, i INF

Read and answer the question below.

1. Informational writing can
   A. share information.
   B. tell how to do something.
   C. explain how something works.
   D. all of the above

Read the paragraph below, and then answer the questions

Gymnastics is a difficult sport. Serious gymnasts must practice for hours a day, several days a week, all year long. This leaves little time for other interests. Gymnasts might want to spend time reading or talking on the phone with friends. Gymnasts are hard on their bodies, and injuries are common. Perfection is important in gymnastics, so practice can be repetitive.

2. What is the main idea?
   A. Gymnastics is a sport for everybody.
   B. Gymnastics is a difficult sport.
   C. Gymnasts often injure themselves.
   D. Sometimes gymnasts even break bones.

3. Which sentence should be deleted from this paragraph?
   A. Gymnastics is a rewarding but difficult sport.
   B. Perfection is important in gymnastics, so practice can be repetitive.
   C. This leaves little time for other interests.
   D. Gymnasts might want to spend time reading or talking on the phone with friends.

4. Which sentence is the best conclusion for this paragraph?
   A. A person needs to truly love gymnastics to stick with it.
   B. Gymnasts are crazy to work so hard.
   C. Gymnastics is a difficult sport.
   D. Great gymnasts can win tournaments and even go to the Olympics.

5. What is the best way to make the following sentence more precise?

   "Gymnasts are hard on their bodies, and injuries are common."

   A. Gymnasts are hard on their bodies.

   B. Gymnasts are hard on their bodies because injuries are common.

   C. Gymnasts are hard on their bodies, and injuries like sprains and fractures are common.

   D. Gymnasts are hard on their bodies, but they take injuries in stride because they love their sport.

Read the following informational writing prompts. Choose one, and write an informational essay. Use the strategies that you learned in this chapter. Use the Student Writing Checklist for Informational Writing to get started and to stay on track.

Prompts:

> You are on a committee that welcomes new students to your school. Write an informational essay that introduces new students to your school. Include information on clubs, sports, school traditions, and other things you think these students should know.

> You are a reporter for your school newspaper. Your assignment this month is to write an essay about a place you have visited. Include information that a visitor would want to know when planning a trip there.

> Your school is encouraging students to become more active. At the start of the school year, a newsletter will go out to all students, describing the extracurricular sports offered at your school. You want to recruit people to your sport. Write an essay that informs readers about your sport and why it is a good one to try.

> Your library is holding an essay-writing contest. Think of a book you've read that you believe everyone in fifth grade should read. Write an informational essay that explains your choice.

Chapter 9
Persuasive Writing

This chapter addresses the Grade 5 Writing Assessment Ideas, Organization, Style, and Conventions rubrics and covers the following GPS standard:

ESL5W2 The student demonstrates competence in a variety of genres.

The student produces a **persuasive essay** that:

a. Engages the reader by establishing a context, creating a speaker's voice, and otherwise developing reader interest.

b. States a clear position in support of a proposal.

c. Supports a position with relevant evidence.

d. Creates an organizing structure appropriate to a specific purpose, audience, and context.

e. Addresses reader concerns

f. Excludes extraneous details and inappropriate information.

g. Provides a sense of closure to the writing.

h. Raises the level of language using appropriate strategies (word choice).

In this chapter, you will review and practice writing a persuasive essay. To see an example of a high-scoring persuasive essay, as well as one that would get a low score, go to chapter 10, Scoring the Essay.

WHAT IS PERSUASIVE WRITING?

Have you ever wanted to persuade someone about something? This means that you wanted to make that person agree with you. Maybe you wanted to convince a friend to do something. Perhaps you wanted your mom or dad to believe that what you were thinking was the best idea.

Persuasion is all around you. Think about the last time you watched television and saw a commercial. The purpose of the commercial was to convince you to buy a product.

Persuasion is also a part of writing. When you do **persuasive writing**, you want to convince readers. To do so, use facts, reasoning, and examples to show that your position is the best choice. In this chapter, you will review how to write a persuasive essay.

PERSUASIVE WRITING CHECKLIST

You may receive a persuasive prompt when you take the Grade 5 Writing Assessment. If you do, you will also get this persuasive writing checklist. It is a good reminder of what you need to do as you write.

Student Writing Checklist for Persuasive Writing

☐ **Prepare Yourself to Write**
Read the writing topic carefully.
Brainstorm for ideas.
Decide what ideas to include and how to organize them.
Write only in English.

☐ **Make Your Paper Meaningful**
Use your knowledge and/or personal experiences that are related to the topic.
Express a clear point of view.
Use details, examples, and reasons to support your point of view.
Organize your ideas in a clear order.
Write a persuasive paper and stay on topic.

☐ **Make Your Paper Interesting to Read**
Think about what would be interesting to your reader.
Use a lively writing voice to hold the interest of your reader.
Use descriptive words.
Use different types of sentences.

☐ **Make Your Paper Easy to Read**
Write in paragraph form.
Use transition words.
Write in complete and correct sentences.
Capitalize, spell, and punctuate correctly.
Make sure your subjects and verbs agree.

WRITING YOUR PERSUASIVE ESSAY

As you work through this chapter, you will draft your own persuasive essay. Choose one of the topics below. Each section of the chapter will tell you what to do next.

Persuasive Essay Topics

- Kids should/should not be able to choose what they eat.

- The best pet for kids to have is _____.

- Kids should/should not get paid to do chores around the house.

- Should there be extra time set aside at school for students to do their homework?

- People should/should not give money to homeless people they run into.

As you write, keep in mind that your biggest goal is to persuade. You want the reader to agree with you. The key to achieving this will be to **support your position**. You will want to include enough details so that your reader feels your argument is strong. You will need to **use persuasive language**. You will need to choose which details are the most important. Let's get started!

Like any other essay, your persuasive essay should have a clear beginning, middle, and end. Your essay will have an introduction, a body, and a conclusion. Think of it as sandwich—bread on top, sandwich fillings in the middle, bread on the bottom.

INTRODUCTION: STATING A POSITION

Persuasive writing begins with a **position**, or a point of persuasion. A position is a stand on an issue. This position becomes the focus of your essay. A good, strong position will make a clear statement that is easy for the reader to understand.

Let's take a look at a sample introduction paragraph for an essay about school uniforms. This writer focuses on the position that students should not be made to wear school uniforms.

> How many things in life do kids get to decide? Bedtime? What to eat? Where to live? If you're like me, then the answer is a big "No!" As kids, we have very little say in our lives. We are told when to sleep, what to eat, and as far as where we live, that's up to our parents. However, at least one thing most of us get to decide is what to wear. I say some of us because many school officials think that, for kids to learn best, they should wear school uniforms. I disagree. Students should not be made to wear school uniforms. We should have the freedom to choose what we wear to school. Making students wear uniforms takes away one of our few decisions, limits creativity, and makes us feel less excited about school.

You will notice in this introduction that the writer began with some questions. These questions help to grab the reader's attention. They also help the reader to understand the writer's position. The writer then states a strong position.

> Students should not be made to wear school uniforms.

There is no mistaking how this student feels! In persuasive writing, it is important for the writer to state the position clearly.

Along with the position, the writer made three points about why uniforms are not a good idea. Those points are:

- Making students wear uniforms takes way one of our few decisions.
- It limits creativity.

- It makes students feel less excited about school.

These points will are important. Each one will become the main idea of one body paragraph.

Practice 1:   Stating a Position

ESL5W2.a, b, d PER

Read each set of statements. Decide which one would best state the position in the introduction, based on the topic given.

1. Topic: The Better Choice for a Pet—Dog or Cat

    A. Dogs are fun and friendly.

    B. It is your choice to own a dog or a cat.

    C. We don't know if a dog or a cat makes the better pet.

    D. Owning a dog is the best choice for any pet lover.

2. Topic: Homework Can Improve Grades

    A. Homework is sometimes very difficult for students to complete.

    B. Doing homework is a good way to help improve your grades.

    C. Homework is not fun, and it takes away time from television.

    D. Without homework to do, students would have more time for family.

3. Topic: Qualities of a Great Friend

    A. A great friend is honest, reliable, and fun.

    B. It is very hard to find a good best friend.

    C. A dog is a man's best friend.

    D. Friendship is an important part of life?

4. Topic: The Importance of Good Nutrition

    A. Good nutrition is an exciting subject because many celebrities like it.

    B. To eat well, you must have the money to buy foods from other countries.

    C. Good nutrition improves your chance to live a long and healthy life.

    D. Exercise is the same thing as good nutrition

5. Now, it's your turn. Consider the topic you picked. Prewrite to get some ideas on paper. Then, draft an introduction. Remember to state your position clearly.

BODY: THREE POINTS TO BACK UP YOUR POSITION

You have stated a position in the introduction. Now, you will move on to the body of your persuasive essay. Use each body paragraph to make a strong point to help convince the reader that your position is right. Your job is to back up your position. Each body paragraph will present **supporting ideas** to show that you are right. You will now expand the three points in your introduction using facts, examples, and good reasoning.

In the example about school uniforms, the writer made these three points:

- Making students wear uniforms takes way one of our few decisions.
- It limits creativity.
- It makes students feel less excited about school.

These points will now be used for the body of the essay.

Practice 2: Three Points to Back up Your Position

ESL5W2.c, d PER

Read each set of sentences and decide which sentence would work best to back up the position.

1. Topic: It is important to eat breakfast every day.

   A. A good breakfast provides energy for the entire day.

   B. Breakfast cereal is a good choice for the morning.

   C. If you miss breakfast, you can always eat a good lunch.

   D. I love to eat waffles and bacon for breakfast.

2. Topic: Encouraging kids to save money is a great way to make them more responsible.

   A. When kids save money, they can buy their own toys and loan money to others.

   B. Kids who save money grow taller and feel more confident.

   C. Children who learn to save grow into adults who continue to save.

   D. Most kids do not get an allowance, so they are not able to save money.

3. Topic: Playing computer games can help students do better in school.

   A. Students enjoy playing computer games for recreation

   B. Students who play computer games get less sleep.

   C. Students can play computer games as a reward for good work in school.

   D. Playing computer games causes many students to rush through homework.

4. Topic: Owning a pet is a great way for a kid to learn responsibility.

    A. Kids who own pets learn to take care of them properly.

    B. Dogs and cats make great pets, but kids need their parents' help with them.

    C. Many kids are allergic to both dogs and cats.

    D. Turtles and gold fish are low maintenance pets for kids to own.

5. Return to your draft introduction. Does it have a thesis? If not, write one with the three points that you want to use. Each point should support your position. You will use these three points as the main ideas for your body paragraphs.

Now, draft your three body paragraphs. Use one of the supporting points in the introduction as the main idea for each body paragraph.

USING PERSUASIVE LANGUAGE

Strong words and phrases are important. **Persuasive language** includes **vivid description**. A reader will pay attention is he or she can picture what you are saying. It also includes **concrete language**. This means that you say exactly what you mean. Instead of something vague like "Some people work harder than others," be more precise. Say, "Some students just do what they have to, while a few take on extra credit projects and go to study groups." When you are supporting a point, be specific.

Finally, use **comparing words** that support your point. Some examples include words that show how you feel about your idea, like *better*, *best*, *more*, *most*, and the like.

Using **logic** and **emotional appeals** will also help to strengthen your language. Using logic means that you explain your points so that your reader will be able to agree and understand them. They really make sense. Here are some examples:

> **Position:** Students should walk rather than run through the school hallways.

Supporting Details Using Logic: When you are running, it is easy to slip and fall. Since this is the case, walking through the school hallways helps cut down on accidents and injuries.

> **Position:** It is better to study first and play later.

Supporting Details Using Logic: When you decide to study before playing, you give yourself a better chance to succeed in school. If you study first, you are able to get your work done early while you are still alert. Your work will be of a better quality. Also, you will be sure to get your study time in before it gets too late and is time to go to bed.

Notice that, in both examples, logical reasons support the details.

Appealing to emotion means that you include details to make people feel a certain way. You might want readers to feel excited about something you find exciting. Or, you might want them to get angry about an issue that upsets you. An emotional appeal can get them to see things your way. Here are some examples:

Position: Littering is bad for the environment
and people.

Emotional Appeal: Think of the beautiful treasures of the earth. There are snow-capped mountains and rolling seas filled with creatures. There are hills covered in soft green grass and colorful flowers that sway in the spring breeze. Imagine a day when all of that beauty has disappeared. If people continue to litter, then one day, it may no longer exist.

In the example above, the writer has done a great job of appealing to the reader's emotion. By using images of beauty, the writer helps the reader to imagine the natural wonders of the world. Then, the writer drives home the point that littering is a danger to and destroyer of this beauty.

Position: Smoking is a dangerous habit and should be avoided
by all.

Emotional Appeal: Smoking is a habit shared by many. Many mothers, fathers, sisters, and brothers—people from all walks of life—fall into a category of smokers. These are the people we love. Yet, their smoking is a dangerous and often deadly habit. What can we do to help save the people we cherish in our lives? We must convince them that their smoking will one day lead them to harm.

In this example, the writer uses the fact that people are attached to their loved ones. This point helps to emphasize the need to avoid smoking.

Practice 3: Persuasive Language

ESL5W2.h PER

For questions 1 and 2, decide which version of the statement uses the most persuasive language. Remember to consider vivid description, concrete language, comparing words, logic, and emotional appeal.

1. A. Athletes earn a lot of money because they are good at their sport.

   B. It's OK that some athletes earn a large amount of money.

   C. Some people think athletes make too much money, but I think there's no problem.

   D. Athletes have short careers, so they need to earn more in the few years they play.

2. A. If you don't have a yard, you can plant flowers or even vegetables in a window container.

    B. The time to plant a window-box garden is in the early spring, when it's getting warm.

    C. A widow-box garden is the best option if you want outdoor plants but have no yard.

    D. When you plant a window-box garden, you can watch from the window as plants grow.

For questions 3 and 4, decide if the writer is using logic or an emotional appeal to persuade the reader.

3. Position: Going to school year round with shorter, more frequent breaks is better than going for nine months and having a long summer break.

    Supporting Detail: A year round schedule with short frequent breaks will mean that teachers and students have time to rest on a regular basis. This would help them by making sure that they are never tired out by long spans of school work.

    A. logic   B. appeal to emotion

4. Position: It is important to know and study your own family history and culture.

    Supporting Detail: Tanya is a lost child. She is an orphan. Tanya is also of mixed heritage. The really sad thing is that she doesn't know anything about her mother or father. She doesn't know her parents. She doesn't know her heritage. Even though Tanya has friends, she sometimes sits and wonders about herself. She wonders about her parents and wishes she could know more about her family history. Maybe one day, she will be able to know more. Until then, she will have to be content with not knowing.

    A. logic

    B. appeal to emotion

5. Take out your draft essay again. Read over your introduction and body paragraphs. Can you improve the language so it is more persuasive? Remember to include vivid description, concrete language, and comparing words. Also look at where you can add logic and emotional appeal to make your point.

PRESENTING THE BEST INFORMATION

In addition to using persuasive language, be sure to develop your ideas with strong details and examples. You will need to present the **best information** in order to convince your reader. Remember to choose the best details to support your position. **Take out extra details** that are off topic.

For example, let's say that the main point you want to make is, "Writing daily is an important part of becoming a good writer." Which sentence would be the best to include in the essay?

A. Writing, like anything else, must be learned and practiced.

B. Many students do not like to write because they rarely do it.

C. People write for many reasons such as to inform, persuade, tell a story, or entertain.

D. Bad writing is very confusing and difficult to read.

If you picked A, then you are correct. Of the choices given, statement A is the best one. While all of the others are about writing, they do not hit the nail on the head as clearly as the first choice. Being a good persuasive writer has a lot to do with being able to choose the very best details to give support to key ideas.

Practice 4: Presenting the Best Information

ESL5W2.c, d, f PER

Decide which detail provides the best support for main points in a persuasive essay. Remember that the writer should leave out any sentences that take the reader off topic.

1. Position: Everyone in a household should be responsible for helping with chores.

   A. There are so many household chores that they could take all day.

   B. Shared responsibility of chores helps to maintain order in the house.

   C. Small babies and young children are not able to help with chores.

   D. The worst chores should be assigned to naughty brothers or sisters.

2. Position: Participating in sports helps students to succeed in school.

   A. Playing sports helps kids to build a sense of confidence and responsibility. This can help when it comes to school work.

   B. Playing sports and going to school can be too much for some students. They can only focus on one thing at a time.

   C. There are so many choices for sporting activities. From basketball to football, swimming, and soccer, there are many possibilities.

   D. I do not like playing sports. It takes time away from family and school work.

3. Position: Kids should be given an allowance.

   A. When kids have money, there are so many neat things to buy.

   B. Giving kids money helps make them smart spenders for life.

   C. Many parents don't like giving their kids allowance.

   D. Allowance should increase with parents' salaries.

4. Position: Kids should own pets.

   A. Poodles are smart pets. Horses are also fun to own.

   B. If you are allergic to cats, you should get a dog.

   C. When kids own pets, they learn responsibility.

   D. Fish do not need a lot of attention.

5. Go back to your draft essay. Have you included the best information to support your position? If you need more details to support your point, add them. Are there extra details that have nothing to do with your argument? If so, delete them.

ANTICIPATING THE READER'S ARGUMENT

Persuasive writing is like writing an argument from just your point of view. You get to present all of your ideas about why your position is right. However, you also have to think about the other side of the argument. If you ignore it, your point will not be as strong. **Anticipating the reader's argument** (the opposite of the view in your paper) is very important. Show that you know what the argument against yours might be. This will make your position more believable because you have thought it through. After you show the opposing point, make a statement to answer the dispute. This way, you are able to weaken the opposing argument and make your position stronger.

Let's practice with some examples.

What argument could be used to dispute this point?

> What you wear is a way to express who you are. Taking away this freedom of expression takes away a part of a kid's identity.

A possible opposing argument:

> There are many ways to express who you are. Wearing clothes of choice is only one of them. If this freedom is taken away, there are many other options for expression.

How could you answer the dispute?

An answer to the opposing argument:

> What are those ways? Kids actually have very few outward ways to express themselves. Most parents don't allow much freedom of hairstyles, makeup, or more permanent decoration either. Clothes seem the best option. Why should this form of identity not be allowed? Shouldn't every person, even kids, have the right to decide how to dress?

Can you think of other points that could answer the dispute?

Let's look at another example.

> Giving kids a choice in their school clothes is one way to help interest them in attending school.

What argument could be used to dispute this point?

A possible opposing argument:

> School is about education. It is not about what students wear or what interests them. Keeping this in mind will make it easier to see that wearing uniforms will not affect what is important about school.

How could you answer the dispute?

An answer to the opposing argument:

> Keeping kids interested in school may not be the main point, but it is still important. Making kids wear uniforms can make them feel like they are in an institution. This casts a negative light on being in school. To help students focus on learning, why not do everything possible to make sure they stay interested? Allowing kids to choose their clothes helps them to stay upbeat about school.

Can you think of other points that could answer the dispute?

Practice 5: Anticipating the Reader's Argument
ESL5W2e PER

Decide which statement could best be used to answer the reader's argument.

Position: Students should get to choose their own seats.

> Reader's argument: Students will choose to sit near their friends and won't pay attention in class.

A. Sitting near friends will help students to pay attention because they want to stay near their friends.

B. It doesn't matter where students sit in the classroom because the teacher can always see them.

C. Students who play around in one seat will play around in another seat.

D. They all answer the reader's argument.

2. Position: People should recycle.

    Reader's argument: Many people are too busy to recycle.

    A. After setting up bins, recycling takes only a few seconds.

    B. In the big scheme of things, recycling is not important.

    C. Recycling can get expensive if the collectors charge fees.

    D. They all answer the reader's argument.

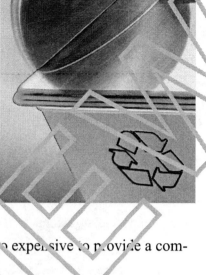

3. Position: Schools should provide computers to every student.

    Reader's argument: It would be too expensive to provide a computer to each student.

    A. Inexpensive computers are available at Wal-Mart.

    B. When it comes to education, quality is more important than expense.

    C. Having a computer would not make any difference in how students learn.

    D. They all answer the reader's argument.

4. Position: Every student should be required to exercise daily.

    Reader's argument: There isn't enough time in the day to require all students to exercise.

    A. Even a small amount of exercise can improve health.

    B. Students could also be given a booklet of exercises to do at home.

    C. At most schools, kids get exercise just walking between classes.

    D. They all answer the reader's argument.

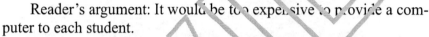

5. Review your draft essay again. Are there possible reader concerns that you can include and answer? If so, add them.

CONCLUSION: WRAPPING UP YOUR ARGUMENT

After you have done your best persuasive writing in the body of your essay, it is time for your conclusion. Your **conclusion** is the finishing touch. It wraps up your ideas and drives home the point you are trying to make. A good conclusion sums up your key points and leaves the reader with something to think about. Let's take a look at a strong conclusion for that persuasive essay about school uniforms.

> Forcing students to wear uniforms takes away one of the few decisions we kids get to make. It also takes away freedom of expression and lowers enthusiasm about school. There could be some guidelines about clothes, so that they are not distracting. But, this can be done without resorting to uniforms. We should do everything possible to make school a place kids want to be. Plus, we should always celebrate our differences. Students should not be forced to wear school uniforms.

Notice that the concluding paragraph brings together all of the strong points. These were set up in the introduction and developed in the body paragraphs. It uses strong language ("Forcing students," "everything possible"), logic ("could be some guidelines…without resorting to uniforms"), and emotional appeal ("we should always celebrate our differences"). It has a strong finish by restating the position ("Students should not be forced to wear school uniforms").

Practice 6: Wrapping up Your Argument

ESL5W2.d, g PER

For each question, choose the best statement to include in the conclusion of an essay about the position given.

1. Position: Owning a pet is a good way for children to learn responsibility.

    A. Hamsters and gerbils make excellent starter pets for most children.

    B. Child pet owners of today are the responsible adults of tomorrow.

    C. The list of chores and responsibilities is long enough already.

    D. The last thing parents need is to have one more thing to supervise.

2. Position: Children can learn good citizenship by helping others.

    A. We already have enough good citizens without adding more to the nation.

    B. There are so many people who need the help of others.

    C. Helping others teaches us that we're all a part of one global community.

    D. One way to reach out and help others is to donate clothes, food, and time.

3. Position: Getting a good night's sleep can help a student to learn more at school.

   A. A good night's sleep is the beginning of fueling for the day ahead.

   B. Without counting sheep or drinking hot milk, it is impossible to get to sleep.

   C. Many kids cannot get a good night's sleep because they are playing video games.

   D. Eating breakfast is just as important as getting a good night's sleep.

4. Write a concluding paragraph for your draft essay. Be sure to sum up your key points and leaves the reader with something to think about.

   When you are finished with your conclusion, check your essay for errors in sentence structure, grammar, spelling, and punctuation. Review chapters 5 and 6 for more about revising and editing. Try scoring your essay using the rubrics in chapter 10.

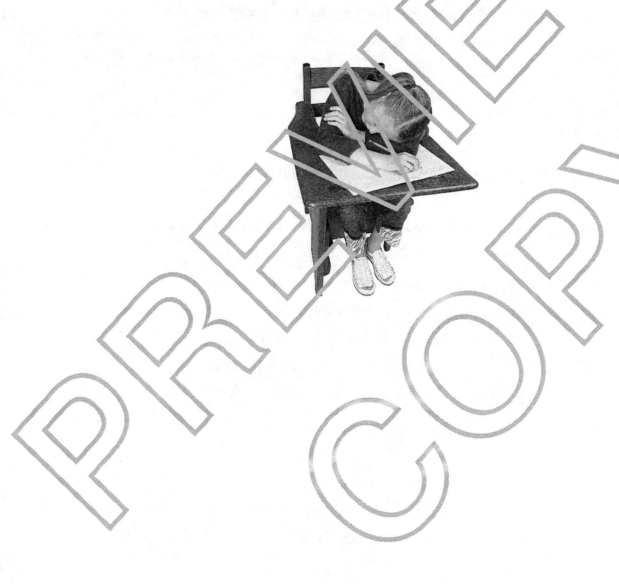

CHAPTER 9 SUMMARY

In **persuasive writing**, the goal is to convince a reader of something. To do this, use facts, details, and examples.

Persuasive writing begins with a **position**. A position is a stand on an issue. The position is the focus of the essay. A good, strong, position will make a clear statement that is easy for the reader to understand.

In the **introduction**, you should state your position. Then, present three points that support the position.

In the **body** of your writing, it is your job to include details that will convince your reader. Each body paragraph develops one of the three points in your introduction.

Use **persuasive language** to help convince your reader that you are right. Remember to include **vivid description**, **concrete language**, and **comparing words**. Using **logic** and **emotional appeals** will also help to strengthen your language.

You will need to present the **best information** possible in order to convince your reader. **Delete extra details** that do not help your argument.

It is important to **anticipate the reader's argument**. It shows that you have thought about all sides. And, answering that argument helps build strong points for persuasion.

A good **conclusion** sums up your key points and leaves the reader with something to think about.

CHAPTER 9 REVIEW

ESL5W2.a, b, c, d, e, f, g, h PER

For questions 1 through 3, decide which sentence makes the best position statement for a persuasive essay.

1. A. Parents should be very involved in their children's education.

    B. What does parent involvement really mean? This is not very clear.

    C. My favorite way to spend time with my parents is through playing games.

    D. Teachers and parents are often very good friends with each other.

2. A. How many seasons are in a year?

    B. A year can be a very long time.

    C. The time in a year flies by very quickly.

    D. Summer is the best season of the year.

3. A. Playing computer games is something that kids and adults enjoy.

    B. Playing computer games has many strong benefits.

    C. Some computer games call for movement and activity.

    D. I do not have a favorite computer game that I like to play.

For questions 4 and 5, decide if the writer uses logic or emotional appeal.

4. Eating fruits and vegetables, drinking water, and getting a good night's sleep are the start of healthful living. A healthy lifestyle is also a happy lifestyle.
    A. logic   B. emotional appeal

5. Friends and family love us the most. If not for ourselves, we can eat and live healthy to be around for those who love us.
    A. logic   B. emotional appeal

For questions 6 through 8, decide which supporting detail is best to include in a body paragraph.

6. Position: Skateboarding as a sport that is great for many kids.

  A. Kids who skateboard learn agility, coordination, and focus.

  B. Kids who skateboard often neglect their homework.

  C. Mothers are afraid that their children will get hurt from skateboarding.

  D. Kids who skateboard are less likely to attend school.

7. Position: Camping teaches survival skills.

  A. Camping can be dangerous and frightening.

  B. Campers must be able to tolerate bugs and animals.

  C. Campers need to know how to make it in the wild.

  D. Camping is difficult in the winter.

8. Position: Kids today do not get enough exercise.

  A. Some kids don't even get thirty minutes of exercise a day.

  B. PE is a time to get in daily exercise. This is a healthy routine.

  C. Kids whose parents don't exercise tend to not get their exercise.

  D. Exercising is a part of healthy living. Diet is a part of healthy living.

For questions 9 and 10, read the position and a possible reader's argument. Decide which answer to the opposing argument would be best to include.

9. Position: Every student should learn to appreciate art, music, languages, and more. There is much to learn beyond the core classes.

    Reader's argument: There are many ways to learn about the world. Art and music doesn't need to be a part of this.

  A. Students become well-rounded if they take art, music, and language classes.

  B. Students who learn to appreciate art become more creative.

  C. One way to get kids involved in art is to have them do art that they enjoy.

  D. none of these

10. Position: Fifth graders are old enough to choose their own bed times.

    Reader's argument: They are too young to be deciding when to go to bed.

    A. Fifth graders are headed toward middle school.

    B. No one should be told when to go to bed.

    C. What is the importance of a bed time?

    D. none of these

For questions 11 and 12, decide which statement would work best as a part of a concluding paragraph.

11. Position: Kids should watch no more than an hour of television each day.

    A. Kids should watch an hour of cartoons on television each day.

    B. The best channel to watch for an hour each day is PBS, which provides educational broadcasting.

    C. Watching more than an hour of television each day takes time away from homework and family.

    D. none of these

12. Position: Kids should have a part in making the rules of the house.

    A. The adults in the house are in charge at all times.

    B. Kids are a part of the house, so they should have a say in the rules.

    C. Many parents refuse to give their children a say in the rules of the house.

    D. none of these

Chapter 10
Scoring the Essay

You will be writing an essay for the Grade 5 Writing Assessment, not scoring it. So, why should you learn how to score? There are two excellent reasons.

First, to do well on the test, you need to review and improve your work. Learning to improve another student's essay will help you improve your own work. Practicing how to revise and edit is a key step. In this chapter, you will read the essays that did not score well. You will have **practice revising and editing** them. You will also read essays that scored high, and they are good examples for you to study.

Second, scoring your own essays and those of other students will help you learn the rubrics. The **scoring rubrics** are lists of what you need to do to score high on the writing test. Read through the rubrics, focusing on what you need to do to score a 5, the highest score. In this chapter, you will practice scoring essays. This will help you learn the rubrics.

You should also return to the essays you wrote for other chapters in this book. Practice scoring each one. Look at what you should improve to get a higher score.

SCORING OF YOUR ESSAY

When you take the Grade 5 Writing Assessment, trained readers will score your essay. Your essay will be scored in four domains (categories): Ideas, Organization, Style, and Conventions. The domains count as follows.

Domain	Domain Value	Calculation of the Score Value
Ideas	40%	2 × grader score
Organization	20%	1 × grader score
Style	20%	1 × grader score
Conventions	20%	1 × grader score

Domains

The **Ideas** domain includes how well your essay focuses on the topic. To score well in this domain, be sure to write the correct type of essay for the prompt you get (narrative, informational, or persuasive). Support your main idea with relevant details. Develop your ideas clearly.

The **Organization** domain scores your overall plan. It looks at with how well you arrange your ideas. Be sure to follow the five-paragraph essay structure. Also, remember to use transitions.

The **Style** domain covers how you capture the reader's attention. This includes word choice, sentence variety, and voice. How precise and vivid is your language? In addition, think about how well you address your audience.

Finally, the **Conventions** domain is all about sentence structure, usage, and mechanics. Check to make sure that all your sentences are correct and clear. Verbs should agree with their subjects. Proofread your essay for spelling, capitalization, and punctuation.

Each domain has five score points. To get the highest score, your essay needs to meet the criteria for score point 5. Read what is needed to score a 5 in each domain.

GEORGIA GRADE 5 WRITING ASSESSMENT: SCORING RUBRICS

> **Domain 1: IDEAS.** The degree to which the writer establishes a controlling idea and elaborates the main points with examples, illustrations, facts, or details that are appropriate to the assigned genre.
>
> Components
>
> - Controlling Idea/Focus
> - Supporting Ideas
> - Relevance of Detail
> - Depth of Development
> - Sense of Completeness
> - Awareness of Genre

5	**Full command of the components of Ideas. The writing is characterized by most or all of the following:**
	• Fully developed controlling idea that addresses all aspects of the assigned writing task
	• Consistent focus on the assigned topic, genre, and purpose
	• Supporting ideas are fully elaborated throughout the paper and relevant to the writer's topic, assigned genre of
	• writing, and audience
	• Response contains specific examples and details that fully address reader concerns and perspectives
4	**Consistent control of the components of Ideas. The writing is characterized by most or all of the following:**
	• Well developed controlling idea that addresses the assigned writing task
	• Consistent focus on the assigned topic, genre, and purpose
	• Supporting ideas and elaboration are relevant to the writer's topic and assigned genre of writing
	• Response contains specific examples and details that address reader concerns and perspectives
3	**Sufficient control of the components of Ideas. The writing is characterized by most or all of the following:**
	• Developed controlling idea that addresses the assigned writing task
	• Generally consistent focus on the assigned topic, genre, and purpose
	• Most supporting ideas are developed and relevant to the writer's topic and assigned genre of writing
	• Some parts of the paper are well developed, while other parts of the paper are only partially developed
	• Response contains sufficient information to address the topic as well as some reader concerns and perspectives
2	**Minimal control of the components of Ideas. The writing is characterized by most or all of the following:**
	• Minimally developed controlling idea that addresses some aspect of the assigned writing task
	• Limited focus on the assigned topic, genre, and purpose
	• Supporting ideas are general and/or under-developed
	• Some ideas may be partially developed, while others are simply listed without development
	• Response lacks sufficient information to provide a sense of completeness
	• Some points and details may be irrelevant or inappropriate for the writer's assigned topic, audience, and genre of writing
1	**Lack of control of the components of Ideas. The writing is characterized by the following:**
	• May announce the topic, but a controlling idea is not established
	• Little or no focus on the assigned topic, genre, and/or purpose
	• Development is lacking due to brevity of the response or unclear supporting ideas
	• Majority of details are irrelevant or the response contains insufficient writing to determine competence in Ideas

Georgia Grade 5 Writing Assessment: Scoring Rubrics

Copyright © American Book Company. DO NOT DUPLICATE. 1-888-264-5877.

> **Domain 2: ORGANIZATION.** The degree to which the writer's ideas are arranged in a clear order and the overall structure of the response is consistent with the assigned genre.
>
> Components
>
> - Overall Plan
> - Introduction/Body/Conclusion
> - Sequence of Ideas
> - Grouping of Ideas
> - Genre-Specific Strategies
> - Transitions

5	**Full command of the components of Organization. The writing is characterized by most or all of the following:** • Overall organizational strategy or structure (introduction, body, and conclusion) is appropriate to the writer's topic and the assigned genre of writing • Logical and appropriate sequencing of ideas within and across parts of the paper • Introduction engages and sets the stage, and conclusion provides a sense of closure • Logical grouping of ideas • Uses effective and varied transitional elements to link all elements of the response: parts of the paper, ideas, paragraphs, and sentences
4	**Consistent control of the components of Organization. The writing is characterized by most or all of the following:** • Overall organizational strategy or structure (introduction, body, and conclusion) is appropriate to the writer's ideas and assigned genre of writing • Logical sequencing of ideas across parts of the paper • Introduction sets the stage, and conclusion ends the piece of writing without repetition • Related ideas are grouped together • Varied transitions link parts of the paper
3	**Sufficient control of the components of Organization. The writing is characterized by most or all of the following:** • Overall organizational strategy (introduction, body, and conclusion) is generally appropriate to the writer's ideas and purpose of the genre • Generally clear sequence of ideas • Introduction is appropriate to the writer's topic and the conclusion is clear • Related ideas generally grouped together • Transitions link parts of the paper
2	**Minimal control of the components of Organization. The writing is characterized by most or all of the following:** • Organizing strategy is formulaic and/or inappropriate to the assigned genre • Minimal evidence of sequencing • May lack an introduction or a conclusion or include an ineffective introduction or conclusion • Unrelated ideas are grouped together • Limited use of transitions (transitions may be formulaic, repetitive, ineffective or overused) • Demonstration of competence limited by the brevity of the response
1	**Lack of control of the components of Organization. The writing is characterized by the following:** • No evidence of an organizing strategy • Unclear sequence of ideas • Lacks an introduction and/or conclusion • Ideas are not arranged in a meaningful order • Lack of transitions or inappropriate transitions • Insufficient writing to determine competence in Organization

GEORGIA GRADE 5 WRITING ASSESSMENT: SCORING RUBRICS

> **Domain 3: STYLE.** The degree to which the writer controls language to engage the reader.
> Components
> - Word Choice
> - Audience Awareness
> - Voice
> - Sentence Variety
> - Strategies Appropriate to the Genre

5	**Full command of the components of Style. The writing is characterized by most or all of the following:** • Carefully crafted phrases or sentences create a sustained tone that engages the reader • Varied, precise, and engaging language that is appropriate to the assigned genre (figurative or technical language may be used for rhetorical effect) • Sustained attention to the audience throughout the paper • Consistent and appropriate voice that is sustained throughout the response • A variety of sentence lengths, structures, and beginnings • A variety of genre-appropriate strategies to engage the reader
4	**Consistent control of the components of Style. The writing is characterized by most or all of the following:** • Language and tone are consistent with the writer's purpose and appropriate to the assigned genre • Word choice is precise and engaging • Attention to audience in the introduction, body, and conclusion • Consistent voice • Sentences vary in length and structure • Some genre-appropriate strategies to engage the reader
3	**Sufficient control of the components of Style. The writing is characterized by most or all of the following:** • Language and tone are generally consistent with the writer's purpose and appropriate to the assigned genre • Word choice is generally engaging with occasional lapses into simple and ordinary language • Awareness of audience demonstrated in the introduction, body, or conclusion • Writer's voice is clear and discernible • Some variation in sentence length and structure • May include some genre-appropriate strategies
2	**Minimal control of the components of Style. The writing is characterized by most or all of the following:** • Language and tone are uneven (appropriate in some parts of the response, but flat throughout most of the response) • Word choice is simple, ordinary and/or repetitive • Limited awareness of audience • Minimal, inconsistent or indistinct voice • Little variation in sentence length and structure • Demonstration of competence limited by the brevity of the response
1	Lack of control of the components of Style. The writing is characterized by the following: • Language and tone are flat and/or inappropriate to the task and reader • Word choice is inaccurate, imprecise, and/or confusing • Little or no attention to audience • Writer's voice is not apparent • Lack of sentence variety • Insufficient writing to determine competence in Style

GEORGIA GRADE 5 WRITING ASSESSMENT: SCORING RUBRICS

Domain 4: CONVENTIONS. The degree to which the writer demonstrates control of sentence formation, usage, and mechanics. *Note: In general, sentence formation and usage are weighted more heavily than mechanics in determining the overall conventions score.*

Components

Sentence Formation	Usage	Mechanics
• correctness	• subject-verb agreement	• internal punctuation
• clarity of meaning	• standard word forms	• spelling
• simple, complex, and compound sentences	• possessives	• paragraph breaks
• end punctuation	• contractions	• capitalization
	• pronoun-antecedent agreement	

5	**Full command of the components of Conventions.** The writing is characterized by most or all of the following: • Clear and correct simple, complex, and compound sentences with correct end punctuation • Correct usage in a variety of contexts • Correct mechanics in a variety of contexts • Errors do not interfere with meaning
4	**Consistent control of the components of Conventions.** The writing is characterized by most or all of the following: • Correct simple, complex, and/or compound sentences with correct end punctuation • Correct usage with some variety of instances but not in all elements • Correct mechanics with some variety of instances but not in all elements • Errors do not interfere with meaning
3	**Sufficient control of the components of Conventions.** The writing is characterized by most or all of the following: • Simple sentences formed correctly, some correct complex and/or compound sentences with occasional errors • Generally correct usage with some errors • Generally correct mechanics with some errors • Few errors interfere with meaning
2	**Minimal control of the components of Conventions.** The writing is characterized by most or all of the following: • Minimal control in the three components of conventions or one component may be strong while the other two are weak • Sentence structure is awkward and/or end punctuation may be missing or incorrect • May have frequent errors in usage and/or mechanics • Some errors may interfere with meaning • Demonstration of competence limited by the brevity of the response
1	Lack of control of the components of Conventions. The writing is characterized by the following: • Frequent sentence fragments, run-ons, and incorrect sentences • End punctuation incorrect or lacking • May contain frequent and severe errors in both usage and mechanics • Errors may interfere with or obscure meaning • Insufficient writing to determine competence in Conventions

SCORING THE NARRATIVE

Let's look at a sample narrative.

Here is the writing prompt:

> Imagine you won a trip for two to anywhere in the world. Write a story telling who you brought with you, where you chose to go, and what you saw and did on your trip.

Now, read one student's response. This example would receive a low score. It has errors in it and does not address the prompt well. We'll use this example to practice scoring and to make some improvements.

One Great Prize!

I went to Italy on vacation one time. It was a good trip. I liked it. Italy is a cuntrey in europe. I rided on a plane for a, long, long, long, time to get there. I road on boats to go from place to place practically every day while I visiting there because there are lots of lakes and rivers in Italy I have always liked riding on boats and in the summertime I spend as much time as I can on my uncle Deans' boat up on Spring lake. I don't think the boats I went on in Italy looked anything like my uncle Dean's boat, but I still really liked riding on them. Plus, it was very hot there and riding on the boat was nicer than walking or riding on a big busy bus. I went on a train to a place where there were no cars at all. No cars allowed! Not ever! People walked whereever they had too go. Sometimes their were goats on the road. I know that some goats are not at all frendly. Also a McDonald's there. I liked my trip. It was good.

What problems do you see in this narrative response? There are quite a few errors.

What do you see right away? There is only one paragraph. This narrative does not follow the five-paragraph format. It does not have a clear beginning, middle, and conclusion. Also, the writer has not told the story in any logical order.

The writer really didn't respond to the prompt. The narrative should be about a prize trip. Instead, the writer throws in all kinds of unrelated ideas about boats, cars, and MacDonald's.

Finally, there are many mistakes in sentence structure, spelling, grammar, and punctuation. All of those need to be fixed. This writer will need to revise and proofread!

Now, try scoring this essay in each of the four domains. Then, work on improving the essay so it can score higher.

Practice 1: Improving the Sample Narrative

A. Practice scoring the sample essay, "One Great Prize!"

1. What score would you give this response in the Ideas domain? Explain why.

2. What score would you give for Organization? Why?

3. What score would you give for Style? Why?

4. What score would you give for Conventions? Provide examples of why you would give this score.

B. Now, revise and edit the essay to improve it.

- Use what you learned in chapters 5 and 6 to revise and edit this essay.
- Refer to chapter 7 for important points about what makes a good narrative.
- Be sure the essay responds to the prompt, follows the five-paragraph format, and is well organized.
- Check the Ideas, Organization, Style, and Conventions rubrics at the beginning of the chapter. Could the essay now score a 5 in each rubric?

Keep your version of this narrative in your writing folder or journal.

C. Now, let's look at another sample narrative written by a student. This one would receive a high score. It responds to the same prompt as the low-scoring essay on page 145. Here is prompt again.

> Imagine you won a trip for two to anywhere in the world. Write a story telling who you brought with you, where you chose to go, and what you saw and did on your trip.

My Prize Trip

I was shocked when my mother told me I won a trip for two to anywhere in the world. I knew exactly where I wanted to go. My Aunt Janie had told me all about the trip she took to Switzerland when she was my age. She described it as the best vacation she had ever taken. So, when my mother asked me where I would like to go, I said, "Switzerland!" Mom thought it was a great idea and she suggested I invite Aunt Janie to go with me.

Aunt Janie and I visited many different places in Switzerland. We visited some big cities that reminded me of the big cities here, complete with tall buildings and lots of traffic. We found a park in one city with a giant chess board. The pieces were so big the tops were higher than my waist. I needed both hands to carry the pieces from space to space!

We also visited several smaller cities, which Aunt Janie called towns and villages. The houses and shops looked like something out of a storybook. They were made of wood with fancy trim, picket fences, and flower gardens. In one village, we watched a man carve a block of wood into the figure of a girl. He sold the figures he carved and painted in his shop. Aunt Janie bought one for me to bring home.

My favorite day was when we traveled up a mountain called Pilates. We rode up the mountain in something called an incline. A special system pulls the car straight up the side of the mountain. When we reached the mountaintop, it no longer looked like summer. Instead of green grass and colorful flowers, everything was white. Two feet of snow covered the ground in every direction! We visited a very unusual house on the mountain. Someone had carved the house, the furniture, and even the dishes from ice! After that, we went on a dog sled ride. Aunt Janie and I sat together in the sled. A driver, or musher, stood behind us and steered and eight huskies pulled the sleigh. I can still feel the bits of snow and ice that pelted our cheeks as we raced across the frozen surface.

Winning that trip was the luckiest thing that ever happened to me. I know that choosing to go to Switzerland and to travel with Aunt Janie were the right choices for me. We saw many interesting things and had lots of fun together. Both Aunt Janie and I agree this was the best vacation trip ever!

You can also practice scoring this essay. Discuss with your teacher what this writer did right to earn a high score.

Scoring the Informational Essay

Now, let's look at an informational essay. Here is the informational prompt:

> Write a report for a friend explaining how to prepare for a test in social studies. Include information about the time and materials needed. Describe each step your friend should take to prepare for the test.

The following essay would not score well. Read it, and decide what needs to be changed to improve this essay.

Tests

I think getting reddy for a social studies test is the same as getting reddy for a test in sience or english but it is difrent then getting reddy for a test in math. I don't like tests. Not in social studies. But I like social studies best. Just not tests. Social studies rules! I like maps. I like globes. I like old stuff. Plus I sit next to my freind in social studies. He is nice. I like sitting next to him. Once we went on a feld trip. To the museum. It was good. But Jon got sick on the bus. That was bad. Once we did a play. I was Abe Linkin. Honest Abe. I wore a big hat. Abe was a Presdent. I wood be a good Presdent. But I wood wear a baseball hat! I think Abe been good in math? I am very good in math too. I always be getting good grades in math. My Mother think I is very smart. Just like Abe!

What's wrong with this essay? First, the writer doesn't answer the prompt. The essay does mention a social studies test. But, most of it talks about what the student likes and doesn't like. It also describes a play, which is totally off the subject. There is no focus on the topic.

This student also seemed to forget five-paragraph essay structure. The writing is not well organized. Also, it is written in narrative style. The writer is telling a story. it should be informational, explaining a process.

What about style? This student use words that are not precise, like stuff, nice, good, and bad. The sentences are short and not varied, and there is a run-on. As for conventions, this paper has many errors. There are spelling problems, and some verbs don't agree with their subjects.

Try scoring this essay yourself. Then, work on improving it so it can score higher.

Practice 2: Improving the Sample Informational Essay

A. Take the sample essay, "Tests," and score it.

1. What score would you give this response in the Ideas domain? Explain why

2. What score would you give for Organization? Why?

3. What score would you give for Style? Why?

4. What score would you give for Conventions? Provide examples of why you would give this score.

B. Now, revise and edit the essay to improve it.

- Use what you learned in chapters 5 and 6 to revise and edit this essay.
- Refer to chapter 8 for important points about what makes a good informational essay.
- Be sure the essay responds to the prompt, follows the five-paragraph format, and is well organized.
- Check the Ideas, Organization, Style, and Conventions rubric at the beginning of the chapter. Could the essay now score a 5 in each rubric?

Keep your improved informational essay in your writing folder or journal.

Look at the next informational essay written by another student. This one would receive a high score. It responds to the same prompt as the low-scoring essay on pages 147–148. Here is prompt again.

> Write a report for a friend explaining how to prepare for a test in social studies. Include information about the time and materials needed. Describe each step your friend should take to prepare for the test.

Getting Ready for a Test

Preparing for a social studies test is not scary if you break it into small steps. The first step begins before the teacher announces the test. Start by reading the chapters when they are assigned. Keep a notebook and pen handy as you read and write an outline of each chapter in the notebook. Use the headings in the text as the main ideas in the outline. Make sure to include every important detail. This will save you time after the test is announced.

Once the teacher tells you the test date, plan for a week of studying. Start by reviewing your outlines. The next day, use the information in the outlines to make flashcards. You will need a stack of 3X5 notecards and a pen. On one side of the card write a question. On the other side of the card, write the answer. Use as many notecards as you need to cover all of the information in your outlines.

The next day, review notes taken in class. Highlight any information in these notes that is not in your outlines. Use the highlighted information to make more flashcards.

On the fourth day, review your flashcards. Place the flashcards question side up. Read the question, and try to answer it. Check your answer with the answer written on the back of the card. Make two separate piles for the cards. Place the cards you answered correctly in one pile, and the questions you got wrong in another pile. Review the questions in the wrong answer pile. Use the flashcards again on the fifth day of studying. Go through the whole pile of cards two or three times, then ask for help. Have a friend or family member quiz you with the cards. Tell them to restate the questions in their own words. This will help because the teacher might not write the questions the same way you did.

The next night, prepare a practice test for yourself. Write one or two questions that can be answered in one or two paragraphs. Then write the answers.

On the last night before the test, review your flashcards once or twice. Then, relax! Get plenty of sleep that night, and in the morning eat a good breakfast.

Following these steps will mean no worrying on the day of the test. You know you are prepared and will probably get a good grade!

C. Try scoring this essay too. Talk with your teacher about what this writer did right to earn a high score.

SCORING THE PERSUASIVE ESSAY

Finally, let's look at a sample persuasive essay. The first example received a low score. It has many errors and lacks focus. Once again, see how you can improve this essay. Here is the prompt:

> Your principal is forming a committee to discuss some needed improvements in your school. The committee will include the principal, some teachers, and one student representative from each grade.
>
> Write a speech to convince your classmates to vote for you as their student representative.

Vote for Me!

I wood be grate on this commitee. I like working on this kind of stuff. I wood make the school change stuff. Like we wood not have homework! We wood have more resess! There wood be no mean teachers. Only fun stuff. All day. Every day. No more tests! No more homework! Just fun fun fun! I will do a grate job. I want to win. So vote for me!

I never been on a committee before. But I want to be. I hate homework! I like the principal. The principal likes me. We is good buddies. I like my techer too. But I hate homework! I rides the bus to school. But I can stay after for this. Only sometimes. I play baseball some days. I am a good baseball player. I play first base. I am on the blue jays. We winned all are games. I love winning! But I hate homework! Maybe we can meet doring school insted. Like doring math. I hate math.

When you read this paper, you can see that the writer missed the point of the prompt. The student talks about the committee but gives few reasons to vote for him/her. There is some unneeded personal information like, "I hate homework!" and "I play baseball some days." It is not clear that this student would make a good committee member. The essay is not convincing.

Consider the rest of the domains as you practice scoring this essay. Then, revise and edit the essay to improve it.

Practice 3: Improving the Sample Persuasive Essay

A. Take the sample essay, "Vote for Me!" and score it.

1. What score would you give this response in the Ideas domain? Explain why.

2. What score would you give for Organization? Why?

3. What score would you give for Style? Why?

4. What score would you give for Conventions? Provide examples of why you would give this score.

B. Now, improve this essay through revising and editing.

- Use what you learned in chapters 5 and 6 to revise and edit this essay.
- Refer to chapters 9 for important points about what makes a good persuasive essay.
- Be sure the essay responds to the prompt, follows the five-paragraph format, and is well organized.
- Check the Ideas, Organization, Style, and Conventions rubrics at the beginning of the chapter. Could the essay now score a 5 in each rubric?

Keep your improved persuasive essay in your writing folder or journal.

Now, read the following persuasive essay. It was written by another student in response to the same prompt as the low-scoring essay on pages 150–151. This essay would receive a high score. Here is prompt again.

> Your principal is forming a committee to discuss some needed improvements in your school. The committee will include the principal, some teachers, and one student representative from each grade.
>
> Write a speech to convince your classmates to vote for you as their student representative.

Why You Should Vote for Me

I will do a great job representing our class on the principal's committee. There are four excellent reasons that a vote for me is really a vote for all of you: I listen carefully, I express my ideas clearly, I get things done, and I really care about our school.

First, I am a great listener. I will listen to your complaints, questions, and concerns with an open mind. The other members of the committee will also have my total attention at meetings. I know if I don't listen carefully to them, I can't do my job and keep you informed. As a peer counselor, I have learned to be a skilled listener. The classes I took and the practice I have had in the Peer-to-Peer program will help me do a great job on the committee.

I am also an experienced speaker. As a volunteer at the zoo, I have had the experience of talking to both large and small groups of people. This experience will help me let the committee know what your problems are and report to you what the committee is doing about them.

My listening and speaking skills also help me to solve problems. I will look at both sides of every problem, and I will try my best to come up with an answer that is fair to everyone. I will treat everyone fairly and not favor one group over another. As a big brother to seven younger brothers and sisters, I have had the chance to solve their problems many times.

The final reason you should vote for me is that I care. I care about our school. I care about our class. I care about all of you. We're all in the same boat, and many of us are friends. I will represent all of you!

So, as you can see, a vote for me is really a vote for you. If I win the election, I will be your eyes and ears on the committee. I will try to act in the way that is best for all of us. The principal's committee is a chance for us to have a say in how things happen in our school, and I hope you all agree that I am an excellent choice for class representative.

C. Try scoring this essay. Discuss with your teacher what this writer did right to earn a high score.

Georgia 5 Writing Assessment Practice Essay Test 1

Imagine that you are taking the Georgia Grade 5 Writing Assessment today. How would you do? What score might your essay get? This practice essay can help you answer these questions. It can show you where you would do well and what you need to work on. The practice essay is based on the Georgia grade 5 scoring rubrics and writing standards.

When you take the Grade 5 Writing Assessment, you will write one essay based on one writing prompt. You won't know what kind of prompt you will get. So, to get the best practice, you should write each kind of essay that you might need to write for the test: narrative, informational, and persuasive. There is one prompt for each type of essay in this test.

How to Use Your Time

To use your time wisely, follow these suggestions:

Planning/Prewriting (15 minutes)

During this time, you will decide what to write. You will use brainstorming or freewriting to generate ideas. You will think quickly to come up with as many ideas as possible. Then, you will organize your ideas and decide what each paragraph will focus on.

Drafting (45 minutes)

You will write your paper in its entirety. In doing so, you will use the best ideas you generated during the planning/prewriting phase.

Revising/Editing (20 minutes)

Now, you will read over what you've drafted. You will revise for organization, making sure that all of your details relate to the main idea. You will add any ideas that are missing, delete anything repetitive or unneeded, improve word choice, and so on. You can also edit any errors in grammar, punctuation, and spelling that you find.

Final Draft (30 minutes)

You will write your final draft neatly. In doing so, you will consider all of the adjustments you have made.

Proofreading (10 minutes)

After writing your final draft, you will proofread for errors in grammar, punctuation, sentence formation, and spelling. This is your final review to ensure that your finished work is your best.

Here are the writing prompts. Use the writing checklist after each prompt. Plan, draft, revise, and edit your response on your own paper. Write a final copy on one clean sheet. Ask your teacher or tutor to tell you when to start and stop writing. Work with your teacher or tutor to score your essay. Use the **Writing Progress Chart** in Appendix C to chart your progress. How did you improve since you wrote the diagnostic essay(s)?

Writing Prompt 1

> Someone is coming to visit your town for the first time. Write a report about the important things to see and do in your town or city. Include any information a visitor would need to enjoy the trip.

Student Writing Checklist for Informational Writing

☐ **Prepare Yourself to Write**
Read the writing topic carefully.
Brainstorm for ideas.
Decide what ideas to include and how to organize them.
Write only in English.

☐ **Make Your Paper Meaningful**
Use your knowledge and/or personal experiences that are related to the topic.
Explain your ideas.
Develop your main idea with supporting details.
Organize your ideas in a clear order.
Write an informational paper and stay on topic.

☐ **Make Your Paper Interesting to Read**
Think about what would be interesting to the reader.
Use a lively writing voice to hold the interest of your reader.
Use descriptive words.
Use different types of sentences.

☐ **Make Your Paper Easy to Read**
Write in paragraph form.
Use transition words.
Write in complete and correct sentences.
Capitalize, spell, and punctuate correctly.
Make sure your subjects and verbs agree.

Writing Prompt 2

Your school is starting a good citizenship program. Each month, one student will receive the Good Citizenship Award. Think about what it means to be a good citizen. Then, write an essay telling who you think should receive the award and why he or she should receive it. Give strong reasons to convince the committee to agree with your choice.

Student Writing Checklist for Persuasive Writing

☐ **Prepare Yourself to Write**
Read the writing topic carefully.
Brainstorm for ideas.
Decide what ideas to include and how to organize them.
Write only in English.

☐ **Make Your Paper Meaningful**
Use your knowledge and/or personal experiences that are related to the topic.
Express a clear point of view.
Use details, examples, and reasons to support your point of view.
Organize your ideas in a clear order.
Write a persuasive paper and stay on topic.

☐ **Make Your Paper Interesting to Read**
Think about what would be interesting to your reader.
Use a lively writing voice to hold the interest of your reader.
Use descriptive words.
Use different types of sentences.

☐ **Make Your Paper Easy to Read**
Write in paragraph form.
Use transition words.
Write in complete and correct sentences.
Capitalize, spell, and punctuate correctly.
Make sure your subjects and verbs agree.

Writing Prompt 3

> Imagine that you changed places with your school's principal for a week. You became the principal and the principal became you. Write a story telling how the change happened and what you would do as principal.

Student Writing Checklist for Narrative Writing

☐ **Prepare Yourself to Write**
Read the writing topic carefully.
Brainstorm for ideas using your imagination and/or personal experiences.
Decide what ideas to include and how to organize them.
Write only in English.

☐ **Make Your Paper Meaningful**
Use your imagination and/or personal experiences to provide specific details.
Tell a complete story.
Create a plot or order of events.
Describe the setting and characters in your story.
Write a story that has a beginning, middle, and end.

☐ **Make Your Paper Interesting to Read**
Think about what would be interesting to the reader.
Use a lively writing voice that holds the interest of your reader.
Use descriptive words
Use different types of sentences.

☐ **Make Your Paper Easy to Read**
Write in paragraph form.
Use transition words.
Write in complete and correct sentences.
Capitalize, spell, and punctuate correctly.
Make sure your subjects and verbs agree.

Georgia 5 Writing Assessment Practice Essay Test 2

Imagine that you are taking the Georgia Grade 5 Writing Assessment today. How would you do? What score might your essay get? This practice essay can help you answer these questions. It can show you where you would do well and what you need to work on. The practice essay is based on the Georgia grade 5 scoring rubrics and writing standards.

When you take the Grade 5 Writing Assessment, you will write one essay based on one writing prompt. You won't know what kind of prompt you will get. So, to get the best practice, you should write each kind of essay that you might need to write for the test: narrative, informational, and persuasive. There is one prompt for each type of essay in this test.

How to Use Your Time

To use your time wisely, follow these suggestions:

Planning/Prewriting (15 minutes)

During this time, you will decide what to write. You will use brainstorming or freewriting to generate ideas. You will think quickly to come up with as many ideas as possible. Then, you will organize your ideas and decide what each paragraph will focus on.

Drafting (45 minutes)

You will write your paper in its entirety. In doing so, you will use the best ideas you generated during the planning/prewriting phase.

Revising/Editing (20 minutes)

Now, you will read over what you've drafted. You will revise for organization, making sure that all of your details relate to the main idea. You will add any ideas that are missing, delete anything repetitive or unneeded, improve word choice, and so on. You can also edit any errors in grammar, punctuation, and spelling that you find.

Final Draft (30 minutes)

You will write your final draft neatly. In doing so, you will consider all of the adjustments you have made.

Proofreading (10 minutes)

After writing your final draft, you will proofread for errors in grammar, punctuation, sentence formation, and spelling. This is your final review to ensure that your finished work is your best.

Here are the writing prompts. Use the writing checklist after each prompt. Plan, draft, revise, and edit your response on your own paper. Write a final copy on one clean sheet. Ask your teacher or tutor to tell you when to start and stop writing. Work with your teacher or tutor to score your essay. Use the **Writing Progress Chart** in Appendix C to chart your progress. How did you improve since you wrote the diagnostic essays and those for Practice Essay Test 1?

Writing Prompt 1

> Imagine an animal followed you home from school one day. Write a speech to persuade your parents or caretakers to allow you to keep the animal as a pet. Give at least three reasons why you should keep the animal.

Student Writing Checklist for Persuasive Writing

☐ **Prepare Yourself to Write**
Read the writing topic carefully.
Brainstorm for ideas.
Decide what ideas to include and how to organize them.
Write only in English.

☐ **Make Your Paper Meaningful**
Use your knowledge and/or personal experiences that are related to the topic.
Express a clear point of view.
Use details, examples, and reasons to support your point of view.
Organize your ideas in a clear order.
Write a persuasive paper and stay on topic.

☐ **Make Your Paper Interesting to Read**
Think about what would be interesting to your reader.
Use a lively writing voice to hold the interest of your reader.
Use descriptive words.
Use different types of sentences.

☐ **Make Your Paper Easy to Read**
Write in paragraph form.
Use transition words.
Write in complete and correct sentences.
Capitalize, spell, and punctuate correctly.
Make sure your subjects and verbs agree.

Writing Prompt 2

> Think about the first memory you have. How old were you? What were you doing? Who were you with? Write an essay to share the memory with your friends. Include many details, so the reader can picture the event.

Student Writing Checklist for Narrative Writing

☐ **Prepare Yourself to Write**
Read the writing topic carefully.
Brainstorm for ideas using your imagination and/or personal experiences.
Decide what ideas to include and how to organize them.
Write only in English.

☐ **Make Your Paper Meaningful**
Use your imagination and/or personal experiences to provide specific details.
Tell a complete story.
Create a plot or order of events.
Describe the setting and characters in your story.
Write a story that has a beginning, middle, and end.

☐ **Make Your Paper Interesting to Read**
Think about what would be interesting to the reader.
Use a lively writing voice that holds the interest of your reader.
Use descriptive words.
Use different types of sentences.

☐ **Make Your Paper Easy to Read**
Write in paragraph form.
Use transition words.
Write in complete and correct sentences.
Capitalize, spell, and punctuate correctly.
Make sure your subjects and verbs agree.

Writing Prompt 3

> Your class is building a display called, "Little Things That Make Life Easier."
> Each member of the class will add one small item and an essay about the item
> to the display. Think about a small item that makes your life easier. Write an
> essay describing the item and telling how the item is used. Explain how it
> makes life easier.

Student Writing Checklist for Informational Writing

☐ **Prepare Yourself to Write**

Read the writing topic carefully.

Brainstorm for ideas.

Decide what ideas to include and how to organize them.

Write only in English.

☐ **Make Your Paper Meaningful**

Use your knowledge and/or personal experiences that are related to the topic.

Explain your ideas.

Develop your main idea with supporting details.

Organize your ideas in a clear order.

Write an informational paper and stay on topic.

☐ **Make Your Paper Interesting to Read**

Think about what would be interesting to the reader.

Use a lively writing voice to hold the interest of your reader.

Use descriptive words.

Use different types of sentences.

☐ **Make Your Paper Easy to Read**

Write in paragraph form.

Use transition words.

Write in complete and correct sentences.

Capitalize, spell, and punctuate correctly.

Make sure your subjects and verbs agree.

Appendix A
Additional Writing Prompts

Narrative Writing Prompts

1. Some people like rainy days, and others like sunny days. What is your favorite kind of weather? Why? Write a story about a perfect day filled with your favorite weather.

2. Write a story based on one of the following:
   - My best talent / skill
   - The best time I ever had with my family
   - The most fun I ever had with my friends
   - I nearly got in trouble that time!
   - My little brother / or / My little sister
   - My big brother / or / My big sister

3. Who is your favorite famous American? Think about famous Americans you know, and choose one. Pretend to be that person, and write a letter or a story as that person. Is the letter or story about a famous event in this person's life, or an ordinary day? Keep in mind how this person might talk and what his or her feelings would be.

4. Write a modern version of a well-known tale. Choose a story you know well. How might the characters be different? What would happen to them? How would the setting be different? Here are a few examples of famous tales, or choose your own: Cinderella, Hansel and Gretel, The Three Little Pigs, Jack and the Beanstalk, Goldilocks and the Three Bears, The Boy Who Cried Wolf.

5. Think about the important people in your life. Write a story about how someone important to you helped you see something new. What did he or she say or do to help you? Tell about the experience.

6. Have you ever done, bought, or worn something just because your friends did? Did you feel pressured to be like your friends? Or is the influence of your friends a positive thing for you? Write about a time when you felt peer pressure. Did you give in to it or not? Was it a positive experience or not?

7. Some days are fun and exciting. Others are boring or filled with bad news. Think about the best day or the worst day you can remember. What happened to make it that way? Tell about that day.

8. Having super powers, like a super hero, could be fun! On the other hand, there would also be great responsibility. If you could have any super power, what would be? Write a story about what power you would have, what you could do, and what you SHOULD do.

9. Think of a place that you have visited (or want to visit) that sticks in your memory. What makes it special? Tell about being in this place.

10. In ancient times, people made up stories about things they did not understand. This included why it was light in the day and dark at night, what made the sound of thunder, and how water came from the sky. Think about something that seems mysterious to you. Write a story to explain how it happens.

Informational Writing Prompts

1. Do you have a favorite saying? Think of a saying that people use often. Or, choose a quote from a famous person. Explain what it means and why you like it. Include details about what makes it special to you.

2. Write instructions for how to do one of the following:
   - Make your own Halloween costume
   - Ride a bicycle
   - Sink a free throw in basketball
   - Fold a paper airplane
   - Cook scrambled eggs

3. Imagine that there is something you want to buy. To do so, you need to earn twenty dollars. You have the idea to sell something at an upcoming block party. What will you make and sell? Write a complete description of how you will plan, what supplies you will need, how you will create your product, and how you will sell enough to make the money you need.

4. What is the best way to make friends? Explain what someone can do to help make new friends.

5. Everyone is afraid or something. Some people are scared of bugs, others don't like heights, and some get very nervous having to talk in front of class. Write about a common fear. Explain why you think people have this fear and some ways to overcome it.

6. Have you ever invented something new? If you haven't, think about something that people need but isn't available in stores. Describe this new product. Tell what it does and who might need it.

7. Think about your favorite possession. Explain what it is and why it is important to you.

8. All through history, there have been many great inventions and discoveries. Many of these changed people's lives forever. Consider the big inventions and discoveries you've learned about. Choose one, and explain how it changed the way we live. Is life better because of it?

9. Have you ever watched a pet grow? For example, you may have had a puppy that grew into a dog or a kitten that became a cat. Or have you watched the life cycle of animals in the classroom, like caterpillars turning to butterflies? Choose an animal that you have observed. Describe how if grows and the stages it goes through. Be specific.

10. A hot topic today is safety on the Internet. Anyone can use the World Wide Web. So, we all have to be careful about inappropriate content. We also need to watch out for computer viruses. Discuss one or more of the risks of the Internet being open to everyone. Talk about what you do, or can do, to be safe on the Web.

Persuasive Writing Prompts

1. A film company is going to make a movie in your town. The producers are looking for extras for a scene that shows families at a fun neighborhood event. Write a letter about yourself and your family. Convince the producers that you should be in this scene.

2. Your parents are limiting your TV privileges. You need to convince them that the shows you like are worth watching. Choose your favorite show, and write about why you should be able to watch it. Be sure to choose three points about what make the show valuable.

3. Your school is looking into adding one new kind of technology to the classrooms. Think all the audio-visual learning tools you have now. Consider what else is needed. What would you like to see added? Write a letter to the principal. Give three reasons why your choice would be the best new technology.

4. Pretend that you and your family could live anywhere. Where would you most want to live? Write an essay describing the best place to live. What three things would be good about it for you and the rest of your family members?

5. Funding is low in your school district. Some sports, music, and arts activities need to be cut. Think about what activities you most enjoy. Write to the Parent-Teacher Association, and convince them that your activity should stay.

6. Have you ever wished you were an adult? Well, a wizard has come to town, and he will turn one child into an adult for a week. What would you want to do that you can't as a kid? Convince the wizard that your wish is an important one and that he should turn you into an adult for a week.

7. Pick a cause that you think is important. Write a public service announcement that convinces people the cause is important. Persuade people to support the cause in some way.

8. Would you rather have more time to do your homework at school? Or would you rather have a shorter school day, with more time for homework at home? Write an article for the school newspaper telling why the school day should be shorter (to allow more time to work at home) or longer (to get more done at school).

9. Choose something in your room at home or something in your locker at school. Write an advertisement that tells how great it is. Give three reasons why people should want to buy it.

10. An old saying reads, "A burden that one chooses is not felt." It means that someone who wants to do a job or take on a responsibility won't look at it as a chore. Agree or disagree with this statement. Give three reasons for your position.

Appendix B
Writing Resources

Web sites

Note: As you know, Web sites tend to change or even disappear over time. American Book Company only suggests the following sites; it is not responsible for any changes that these sites may make in content or intent.

These Web sites include a variety of information with links to still more sites designed as supplemental aids for students. We visited these sites and devised a rating system for them.

Ratings	
Excellent	★ ★ ★ ★
Good	★ ★ ★
Fair	★ ★
Poor	★

Ask Miss Grammar

First, ignore the silly cartoon lady. When you do that, this site does have a lot going for it. There is an option to look through "archives," where you select an item you wish to learn more about. You can also bring up facts and games. Or, you can choose the option to e-mail a specific question to the site. The site states that it cannot answer all e-mail, but it tries to answer many.

Web address

http://www.protrainco.com/grammar.htm

Rating

 ★ ★ ★

ESL Home Page

The ESL Home Page is a great starting place for ESL and ELL students working on the Web. It contains many links to the areas of study that any student can use. There are also ESL chat rooms. The best features are the grammar and writing games and activities. Some possibilities are links on the left-hand side about writing, grammar, idioms, and more.

Web address   **Rating**

http://www.rong-chang.com/   ★ ★ ★

Interesting Things for ESL Students

This site is designed for ESL students, but native English speakers may use its many activities to sharpen English skills too. The site is filled with a variety of quizzes, word games, word puzzles, anagrams, lessons, and a random sentence generator. The interactive pages tell whether they require Flash, Java, or Javascript technology. Links are included to free download sites for the required software.

Web address   **Rating**

http://www.manythings.org   ★ ★ ☆

Paradigm: Online Writing Assistant

This site features discussions about how to write essays. It also has good tips for revising and editing. The site is clearly written and organized. This is a good source for those who want a review of the composition process.

Web address   **Rating**

http://www.manythings.org/   ★ ★ ★

Books and Software

This section contains a listing of books which provide students with grammar and writing instruction in various formats.

Basics Made Easy: Grammar and Usage Review

This book provides clear explanations and plentiful practice exercises on grammar, punctuation, and usage. Chapter reviews reinforce concepts taught in each lesson. The book is a thorough and excellent support for aspiring writers.

Pintozzi, Frank, and Devin Pintozzi. *Basics Made Easy: Grammar and Usage Review.* Woodstock, GA: American Book Co., 1998, revised 2007.

Web address www.americanbookcompany.com

Basics Made Easy: Grammar and Usage Software

This interactive software program offers a comprehensive review for grammar, punctuation and usage. Exercises require students to choose the best answers. The software tracks students' scores and correlates with lessons in the companion text, *Basics Made Easy: Grammar and Usage Review* (American Book Company).

Pintozzi, Frank, and Devin Pintozzi. *Basics Made Easy: Grammar and Usage Software.* Woodstock, GA: American Book Co., 2000.

Web address www.americanbookcompany.com

Focus: From Paragraph to Essay

The author presents a practical and easy to read text about writing and grammar. She includes plenty of exercises. There are also writing topics and examples of student writing.

Campbell, Martha E. Focus: From Paragraph to Essay. Upper Saddle River, NJ: Prentice Hall, 1996.

Writer's Choice: Grammar and Composition

This text contains lessons in writing, grammar, resources, and literature. The writing activities are helpful for improving skills.

Royster, Jacqueline Jones, et al. *Writer's Choice: Grammar and Composition.* New York: McGraw-Hill, 1996.

A Writer's Guide to Transitional Words and Expressions

This book is a helpful companion reference to *A Writer's Guide to Using Eight Methods of Transition* (see below). It contains over 1000 transitional words and expressions. Using these can help make your writing more effective, logical, and easy to read.

Pellegrino, Victor C. *A Writer's Guide to Transitional Words and Expressions.* Wailuku, HW: Maui Arthoughts, 1987.

A Writer's Guide to Using Eight Methods of Transition

This brief but excellent guide helps writers choose the best transitional words and expressions for a context. The author provides many examples of connecting sentences and paragraphs.

Pellegrino, Victor C. *A Writer's Guide to Using Eight Methods of Transition.* Wailuku, HI: Maui Arthoughts, 1987

Writing from A to Z: The Easy-to-Use Reference Handbook

This book is organized alphabetically like a dictionary. So, students can easily find, for example, an explanation of a "paragraph" by looking in the letter "P"section. The book covers a wide range of grammar and usage information.

Ebest, Sally Barr. *Writing From A to Z: The Easy-to-Use Reference Handbook.* Mountain View, CA: Mayfield, 1997.

Writing Talk: Sentences and Paragraphs with Readings

A work book that is too good to be a work book, *Writing Talk* is worth its weight in good grades for its readings alone. It also has a thorough review of basic concepts and instruction written with wit and an understanding of how to build the skill of writing.

Winkler, Anthony C. and Jo Ray Mccuen-Metherell. *Writing Talk: Sentences and Paragraphs with Readings*. 3rd ed. Upper Saddle River, NJ: Prentice Hall, 2003.

Writing Talk: Paragraphs and Short Essays with Readings

This is the second volume of the *Writing Talk* book series. See above for comments.

Winkler, Anthony C. and Jo Ray Mccuen-Metherell. *Writing Talk: Sentences and Paragraphs with Readings*. 3rd ed. Upper Saddle River, NJ: Prentice Hall, 2003.

The Young Person's Guide to Becoming a Writer

Reading this book will be a different experience from reading the others. This guide is gently encouraging to students who want to pursue a career in writing but are not sure how to take the first steps. There are sections on writing skills, literary genres, and how to keep a writer's notebook. This is a first look into the world of professional writing, and it is good for everyone to know the ways to enter that world.

Grant, Janet E. *The Young Person's Guide to Becoming a Writer*. Minneapolis: Free Spirit, 1995.

Appendix C
Student Essays Progress Chart

Keep all of your essays in a folder. This can include those you worked on throughout this book. It can also include any you wrote for practice from the prompts in Appendix A.

As you practice, use the chart below to track your progress. For each essay, work with your teacher or tutor to grade your work. If you have an excellent grasp of the skill, write **E for Excellent**. If you use the skill well enough to pass, but you could improve even more, write **P for Passing**. If you need to practice a skill more to master it, write **NP for Needs Practice**.

For any skill marked **NP**, study the chapter that reviews that skill. Be sure to complete the practices in that chapter. Then, do the same for skills marked **P** after studying these chapters, practice by writing more essays (using the prompts in Appendix A). Evaluate your progress again.

Writing Skills	Chapter Number	Student Name:					
		Essay 1	Essay 2	Essay 3	Essay 4	Essay 5	Essay 6
Correctly uses parts of speech	1						
Effective sentence structure	2						
Correct sentence punctuation	2						
Sentence variety	2						
Generating and organizing ideas	3						
Appropriate focus and purpose	3						
Five-paragraph structure	4						
Effective introduction	4						
Well-developed body paragraphs	4						
Effective conclusion	4						
Coherence and good transitions	5						
Consistent tone and voice	5						
Editing for conventions	6						
Qualities of effective narrative	7						
Qualities of effective informational essay	8						
Qualities of effective persuasive essay	9						

CRCT

Please fill out the form completely, and return by mail or fax to American Book Company.

Purchase Order #: _____   Date: _____

Contact Person: _____

School Name (and District, if any): _____

Billing Address: _____   Street Address: _____ ☐ same as billing

_____   _____

Attn: _____   Attn: _____

_____   _____

_____   _____

Phone: _____   E-Mail: _____

Credit Card #: _____   Exp Date: _____

Authorized Signature: _____

Order Number	Product Title	Pricing* (10 books)	Qty	Pricing (30+ books)	Qty	Total Cost
GA1-R0409	Mastering the Georgia 1st Grade CRCT in Reading	$169.90 (1 set of 10 books)		$329.70 (1 set of 30 books)		
GA2-M0409	Mastering the Georgia 2nd Grade CRCT in Science	$169.90 (1 set of 10 books)		$329.70 (1 set of 30 books)		
GA2-H0409	Our State of Georgia (2nd Grade Social Studies)	$169.90 (1 set of 10 books)		$329.70 (1 set of 30 books)		
GA3-M0607	Mastering the Georgia 3rd Grade CRCT in Math	$169.90 (1 set of 10 books)		$329.70 (1 set of 30 books)		
GA3-R0607	Mastering the Georgia 3rd Grade CRCT in Reading	$169.90 (1 set of 10 books)		$329.70 (1 set of 30 books)		
GA3-S0508	Mastering the Georgia 3rd Grade CRCT in Science	$169.90 (1 set of 10 books)		$329.70 (1 set of 30 books)		
GA3-H1008	Mastering the Georgia 3rd Grade CRCT in Social Studies	$169.90 (1 set of 10 books)		$329.70 (1 set of 30 books)		
GA4-M0808	Mastering the Georgia 4th Grade CRCT in Math	$169.90 (1 set of 10 books)		$329.70 (1 set of 30 books)		
GA4-R0808	Mastering the Georgia 4th Grade CRCT in Reading	$169.90 (1 set of 10 books)		$329.70 (1 set of 30 books)		
GA4-S0708	Mastering the Georgia 4th Grade CRCT in Science	$169.90 (1 set of 10 books)		$329.70 (1 set of 30 books)		
GA4-H1008	Mastering the Georgia 4th Grade CRCT in Social Studies	$169.90 (1 set of 10 books)		$329.70 (1 set of 30 books)		
GA5-M0806	Mastering the Georgia 5th Grade CRCT in Math	$169.90 (1 set of 10 books)		$329.70 (1 set of 30 books)		
GA5-R1206	Mastering the Georgia 5th Grade CRCT in Reading	$169.90 (1 set of 10 books)		$329.70 (1 set of 30 books)		
GA5-S1107	Mastering the Georgia 5th Grade CRCT in Science	$169.90 (1 set of 10 books)		$329.70 (1 set of 30 books)		
GA5-H0808	Mastering the Georgia 5th Grade CRCT in Social Studies	$169.90 (1 set of 10 books)		$329.70 (1 set of 30 books)		
GA5-W1008	Mastering the Georgia Grade 5 Writing Assessment	$169.90 (1 set of 10 books)		$329.70 (1 set of 30 books)		
GA6-L0508	Mastering the Georgia 6th Grade CRCT in ELA	$169.90 (1 set of 10 books)		$329.70 (1 set of 30 books)		
GA6-M0305	Mastering the Georgia 6th Grade CRCT in Math	$169.90 (1 set of 10 books)		$329.70 (1 set of 30 books)		
GA6-R0108	Mastering the Georgia 6th Grade CRCT in Reading	$169.90 (1 set of 10 books)		$329.70 (1 set of 30 books)		
GA6-S1206	Mastering the Georgia 6th Grade CRCT in Science	$169.90 (1 set of 10 books)		$329.70 (1 set of 30 books)		
GA6-H0208	Mastering the Georgia 6th Grade CRCT in Social Studies	$169.90 (1 set of 10 books)		$329.70 (1 set of 30 books)		
GA7-L0508	Mastering the Georgia 7th Grade CRCT in ELA	$169.90 (1 set of 10 books)		$329.70 (1 set of 30 books)		
GA7-M0305	Mastering the Georgia 7th Grade CRCT in Math	$169.90 (1 set of 10 books)		$329.70 (1 set of 30 books)		
GA7-R0707	Mastering the Georgia 7th Grade CRCT in Reading	$169.90 (1 set of 10 books)		$329.70 (1 set of 30 books)		
GA7-S1206	Mastering the Georgia 7th Grade CRCT in Science	$169.90 (1 set of 10 books)		$329.70 (1 set of 30 books)		
GA7-H0208	Mastering the Georgia 7th Grade CRCT in Social Studies	$169.90 (1 set of 10 books)		$329.70 (1 set of 30 books)		
GA8-L0505	Passing the Georgia 8th Grade CRCT in ELA	$169.90 (1 set of 10 books)		$329.70 (1 set of 30 books)		
GA8-MATH08	Passing the Georgia 8th Grade CRCT in Math	$169.90 (1 set of 10 books)		$329.70 (1 set of 30 books)		
GA8-R0505	Passing the Georgia 8th Grade CRCT in Reading	$169.90 (1 set of 10 books)		$329.70 (1 set of 30 books)		
GA8-S0707	Passing the Georgia 8th Grade CRCT in Science	$169.90 (1 set of 10 books)		$329.70 (1 set of 30 books)		
GA8-H0607	Passing the Georgia 8th Grade CRCT in Georgia Studies	$169.90 (1 set of 10 books)		$329.70 (1 set of 30 books)		
GA8-W0907	Passing the Georgia Grade 8 Writing Assessment	$169.90 (1 set of 10 books)		$329.70 (1 set of 30 books)		

1-5-09   *Minimum order is 1 set of 10 books of the same subject.

Subtotal _____

Shipping & Handling 12% _____

Total _____

American Book Company ● PO Box 2638 ● Woodstock, GA 30188-1383
Toll Free Phone: 1-888-264-5877 ● Toll-Free Fax: 1-866-827-3240
Web Site: www.americanbookcompany.com

Call Toll-Free 1-888-264-5877 to ORDER and for FREE PREVIEW COPIES!

Visit americanbookcompany.com to download FREE SAMPLES of all of our products!